Contents

Welcome to *The Week Junior Annual 2018*

Every page is packed with fascinating facts and need-to-know information.
Tick off each feature when you've read it.

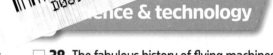

ROVING REPORTER

Send your news, jokes and photos to hello@ theweekjunior.uk. If they're printed in the magazine you'll win a Roving Reporter badge.

Editor Anna Bassi
Deputy editor Felicity Capon
Staff writers Stevie Derrick, Augustin Macellari, Chloe Ward
Editorial assistant Kaye O'Doherty
Art editor Dave Kelsall
Picture editor Colin Williams
Production editor Vanessa Harriss
Sub-editor Hugh Porter
Contributors Dan Green, Alex Peake-Tomkinson, Kevin Pettman, Simon Ward, Katherine Woodfine
Digital Production Manager Nicky Baker

Management
Magbook publisher Dharmesh Mistry
Operations director Robin Ryan
Newstrade director David Barker
Publisher and chief executive, The Week Kerin O'Connor
Chief operating officer Brett Reynolds
Chief executive James Tye
Company founder Felix Dennis
All material © Dennis Publishing Ltd, 31–32 Alfred Place, London WC1E 7DP. The Week and The Week Junior are registered trademarks of Felix Dennis. The Week Junior is licensed to The Week Ltd by Dennis Publishing Ltd. The contents of this annual may not be reproduced in whole or part without the consent of the publishers

The Week Junior Annual 2018 ISBN 978-1-78106-559-4

Licensing & Syndication
To license this product please contact Carlotta Serantoni at carlotta_serantoni@dennis.co.uk To syndicate content from this product please contact Ryan Chambers at ryan_chambers@dennis.co.uk

Liability
While every care was taken during the production of this annual, the publishers cannot be held responsible for the accuracy of the information or any consequence arising from it. The paper used within this annual is produced from sustainable fibre, manufactured by mills with a valid chain of custody. Printed at Buxton Press

THE WEEK Junior

Dennis

British Media Awards
PRINT PRODUCT OF THE YEAR 2017

British Media Awards
BEST NEW LAUNCH 2016

Talent AWARDS
BEST ART TEAM 2017

BRITISH MAGAZINE EDITORS
LAUNCH OF THE YEAR 2016

20 questions

Spend a few minutes filling in the answers to our 20 questions. When you look at your book in years to come, it'll be a great way to help you remember what it was like to be you in 2018.

Start here...

1. My age ☐   2. Today's date ☐

3. Where are you sitting right now?

_____

_____

_____

4. What are you wearing? Describe your outfit and draw a picture, too.

_____

_____

_____

5. What was the last thing you did before doing this?

_____

_____

_____

6. Who was the last person you spoke to?

7. Name the best book you read last year.

_____

8. Who is your favourite singer or band?

_____

9. Which film did you most enjoy watching in 2017?

_____

10. What would be your personal theme tune?

_____

11. What would be your superpower?

_____

_____

_____

Draw Super You here...

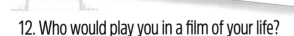

12. Who would play you in a film of your life?

_____

13. What is the best thing about being you?

_____

_____

_____

14. What's your favourite sandwich filling?

_____

WOW!
The record for the world's biggest sandwich belongs to Wild Woody's Chill and Grill, Michigan, US. It was 3.6 metres square, and its fillings included around 468 kilograms of corned beef, 118 kilograms of cheese and 68 kilograms of mustard.

15. What's your favourite word?

_____

16. If you could do one thing to change the world, what would it be?

_____

_____

17. What are you most proud of?

_____

_____

18. What makes you happy?

_____

19. What's your favourite smell?

_____

_____

DID YOU KNOW?
The scent of lavender is supposed to help you sleep; a zesty lemon fragrance can make you feel more alert.

20. What three things would you like to achieve before your next birthday?

1.
_____

2.
_____

3.
_____

INDIA'S ANCIENT STEPWELLS

In the northern Indian states of Rajasthan and Gujarat, hundreds of ancient wells, like this one, can be found. Some date back to AD550. They used to be used for drinking, bathing, prayer and meditation, but today, many have run dry and are no longer used.

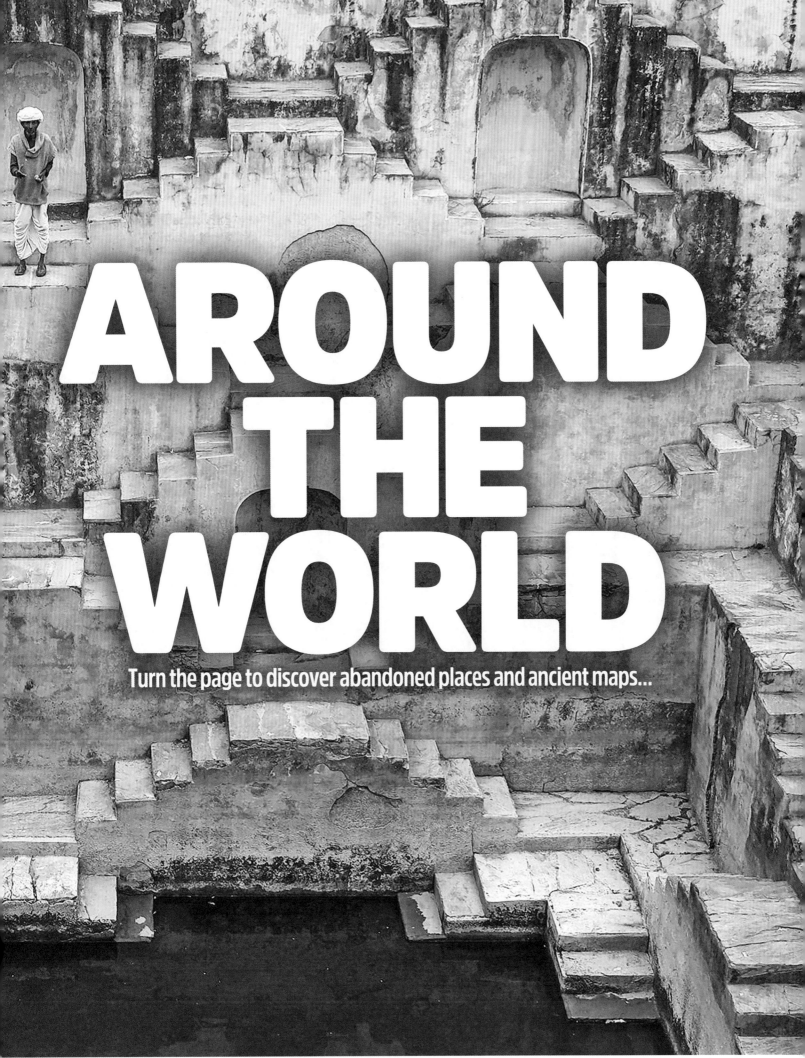

AROUND THE WORLD

Turn the page to discover abandoned places and ancient maps...

Mapping the globe

From ancient clay tiles to modern-day GPS, what do maps tell us about humans?

You might think that a map is nothing more than a drawing of a particular area, such as a city, country or continent. Maps tell us about our surroundings and are important tools to make sure we don't get lost. Throughout history maps have been created for all sorts of reasons. Maps don't just tell us about borders and territories, they tell us how humans think, feel and live.

The very first maps

The history of maps goes back more than 5,000 years. The earliest surviving map of the world is a clay tablet from Babylon. The ancient city of Babylon was the centre of civilisation for roughly two millennia. Its location was around 60 miles south of Baghdad, in modern Iraq. The map dates back to the 6th century BC and shows Babylon in the centre, the River Euphrates, and the surrounding ocean and mountains.

One of the world's earliest maps.

WHOOPS!
An early Spanish explorer reported in the 16th century that California, in the US, had water on all sides. He'd made a mistake, but California was drawn as an island well into the 18th century as a result.

DID YOU KNOW?
Cartography is the name given to the science or art of making maps.

Introducing Ptolemy

The people of ancient Greece and the Romans made maps. However, it was Claudius Ptolemy (pronounced Tollemmy; the P is silent) who changed them forever. Ptolemy was an astronomer, geographer and mathematician who lived in Egypt at the time of the Romans in the 2nd century AD. His work relied on mathematics and geometry. He plotted about 10,000 locations by creating a system that used imaginary lines known today as latitude and longitude.

Latitude and longitude

Ptolemy, like the Greeks and Romans of the time, knew the Earth was round, not flat. But how could he draw the planet's spherical surface onto a flat sheet of paper? Imaginary lines across the Earth's surface, known as latitude and longitude, were the answer. Parallel lines of latitude circle the Earth in an east-west direction; lines of longitude run from the North Pole to the South Pole. Together they turn the Earth's surface into a grid. Latitude and longitude are still used today to plot locations on a map.

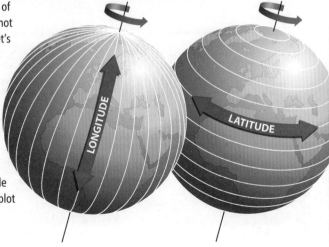

The Renaissance

The Renaissance was a period in European civilisation between the 15th and 17th centuries. During this time, new inventions and ideas were changing the world. Ships were crossing oceans and countries were building empires; so accurate maps were vital. Mapmakers were influenced by Ptolemy's ideas about latitude and longitude and the invention of the printing press in around 1440 meant that monasteries were no longer the only places that could produce maps.

Modern maps

Today, advances in technology have made maps more reliable than ever. This is thanks to GPS, which stands for Global Positioning System, which uses satellites in space set up by the US military. Most people find their way around using GPS on their smartphones. However, some experts worry that our blind trust in technology means we are losing our natural sense of direction. There have been reports of people driving into lakes, deserts, and even other countries by mistake, after following the instructions on their devices. Perhaps we're no smarter than the Babylonians after all.

Maps help us to understand our world.

After the Roman Empire

After the fall of the Roman Empire, maps made in Europe became more about storytelling. They were often made in monasteries, and showed biblical events. The Mappa Mundi (map of the world), which dates from the 1290s, shows Noah's Ark, Adam and Eve and strange creatures. Mapmakers put what was most important to them at the centre. One map, by the Muslim cartographer Muhammad al-Idrisi, placed Mecca, the holiest city in the religion of Islam, at the centre of the world.

The Mappa Mundi.

Time for prayer
Millions of Muslims travel to Mecca, in Saudi Arabia, each year.

Traffic jam
Rush hour in Ho Chi Minh City, Vietnam.

MASSIVE STATE
Texas is the second largest state in the US, and bigger than almost every country in Europe (only the European part of Russia is bigger).

Stuck in the mud
Cadillac Ranch is an art installation created from vintage Cadillac cars in a corn field near Amarillo, Texas.

City view
The Park Güell in Barcelona was designed by architect Antoni Gaudí. The entrance is guarded by a mosaic dragon.

Busy as a bee
Bee-keepers at work in Mombasa, Kenya.

Thundering torrent
People visit the Hukou Waterfall on the Yellow River in China. In August 2017, because of heavy rain, the volume of water surged.

DID YOU KNOW?
It is called the Yellow River because it contains a large amount of fine, mineral-rich silt that turns the water a yellowy colour.

Rainbow walk
Artist Darko Caramello Nikolic creates works that allow people to explore colours and forms, such as this walkway in Hanover in Germany.

Thirsty work
A traditional Berber water seller in Morocco. Their water bags are made from goat hide.

EARTH'S AMAZING ABANDONED PLACES

Find out why these strange locations are no-go areas.

The global population is expected to hit eight billion by 2023. That's a lot of people, most of whom live in hectic, sprawling cities. Yet there are also places on Earth that for one reason or another have been abandoned by humans, and are eerily quiet. Here are the incredible stories behind these deserted destinations.

Monuments to dead technology

At certain points on England's coastline can be found huge, mysterious concrete structures. These large half-spheres, some twice the height of a London bus, look like alien monuments angled out to sea. Some of the most notable are on Romney Marsh, in Kent, where they sit upon Greatstone Lakes. The vast concrete forms were in fact supposed to give an early warning of approaching enemy aircraft. Built between 1928 and 1930, they were designed to pick up the distant sounds of engines by catching the sound and focusing it on a precisely placed microphone in its centre. They fell into disuse with the invention of new technology, and now are relics of the past.

Pripyat, Ukraine

The radioactive town

The city of Pripyat was built especially to house the workers of a nearby nuclear power station, Chernobyl. It was founded in 1970, and by 1986 had a population of around 30,000 people. On 27 April 1986, all of its inhabitants abandoned the city, along with their possessions – never to return. A day earlier, explosions had torn through Chernobyl Nuclear Power Plant, in what has been recognised as the biggest nuclear disaster of all time. Toxic levels of radiation, a kind of harmful energy, poured out of the power plant. Now, the town has been reclaimed by nature, and plants and trees grow where humans once lived and worked.

AS SEEN ON SCREEN
You don't have to go all the way to Japan to see a Bond location; the Eden Project in Cornwall was also used as a baddie's lair, in *Die Another Day.*

An abandoned funfair at Pripyat.

Hashima Island, Japan

A Bond villain's lair

The eerie island of Hashima, off the coast of Japan, may look familiar. That's because it made an appearance in the James Bond film, *Skyfall*, where it was used as the villain's remote hideaway. Also known as Battleship Island, for much of the 20th century it was home to thousands of miners and their families. The miners dug coal from beneath the island – at the industry's peak they produced 400,000 tonnes every year. As the coal ran low, and Japan switched to oil for fuel, the mine was shut. By 1974, the island was abandoned. Now, guided tours take tourists to experience its atmosphere.

Snakes have overrun the island.

Ilha de Queimada Grande, Brazil

Island of the snakes

Although it seems like an idyllic paradise, Ilha de Queimada Grande is not the sort of place you'd like to visit. It's completely unfit for human habitation, thanks to the thousands and thousands of deadly golden lancehead vipers that infest the island. It's thought the snakes were trapped there 11,000 years ago, when the rising sea level cut it off from the mainland. The snakes evolved separately from their cousins on the mainland, and now, without any natural predators, they have the run of the island – some say that there's a snake per square metre. Yikes!

Michigan Central Station, US

The last train has long since left

In the late 20th century, the city of Detroit, in Michigan, US, suffered a serious decline. As the centre of US car manufacturing it had been rich. With foreign companies competing for business, however, the US car industry began to struggle – and so did Detroit. Many people left the city and it declared itself bankrupt (unable to pay back the money it owed) in 2013. One reminder of the city's decline is Michigan Central Station. It was the tallest railway station in the world when it was built in 1913, but the last train departed in 1988. It has been empty ever since.

Kolmanskop, Namibia

Reclaimed by the dunes

In the dry and dusty Namib desert sits the uninhabited town of Kolmanskop. In this once rich and bustling town, with its own bowling alley, theatre and hospital, all that remains are grand old houses slowly filling with sand. The village was home to rich miners, who made their money from the diamonds they dug up in the area. As the diamonds ran out, the miners left, until in 1954 the town was finally abandoned.

An appetite for adventure

Ben Fogle reveals what makes him tick.

Ben Fogle loves the wilderness.

For more than 17 years, Ben Fogle has been a familiar face on UK television. Since 2000, he's rarely been off our screens. He's known for his extraordinary adventures and feats of endurance. He's trekked more than 400 miles through one of the most inhospitable deserts, raced over the frozen continent of Antarctica and rowed across the Atlantic Ocean.

Fogle grew up in London, with his mum, dad and two sisters. His father was a vet, and the family lived above his surgery. Sometimes, when Fogle got home from school, he'd see his dad at work – performing operations on different creatures. The family also shared the house with animals; they had a couple of dogs, as well as Humphrey, an African grey parrot. Fogle's mother was an actor, and so he was used to famous people dropping in at his house.

OFF-LIMITS
His family has always supported Fogle when it comes to his adventures – but there's one place that's a no-go area. They won't let him climb Everest because it's just too dangerous.

Childhood trips to Canada, where his father grew up, inspired Fogle's love of the outdoors – but it was during his gap year, after he finished school, that he discovered his passion for travel. South America left him wide-eyed with wonder. "For me it was the first time I'd seen totally different cultures," he remembers. "The smells, the colours, everything about it was rich and vibrant."

Since those days, Fogle has travelled to more of the world's countries than you can count, to rainforests and remote islands.

If he didn't live in the UK, he imagines himself "somewhere in a tent, most likely Africa or South America". If his job hadn't led him all over the world, he says, he'd have gone there himself, "working for an NGO (non-governmental organisation, such as a charity) somewhere". For now, he says, "I am never happier than when I am in the wilderness."

CREATURE COMFORTS
When Fogle went to the remote island of Taransay in the Outer Hebrides for *Castaway 2000*, he was allowed to take one luxury item. He took Inca, his beloved labrador puppy.

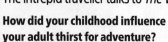

INTERVIEW

Ben Fogle

The intrepid traveller talks to *The Week Junior* about adventures, scuba diving and snotcicles.

How did your childhood influence your adult thirst for adventure?
I spent a great deal of my childhood in the Canadian wilderness. My father is Canadian and he gave us long summers in the Canadian wilds – canoeing, fishing, camping and watching the native wildlife.

You've had countless amazing adventures. Which was the best?
The best was living for a year on an uninhabited island in the Outer Hebrides, in Scotland. I lived there with 30 other people as part of a reality

TV show, called *Castaway 2000*. We had to create a fully self-sufficient community there. There were kids, too. They loved it.

Which was the toughest adventure?
The coldest was walking to the South Pole. It got down to -70°C; my snot froze, forming snotcicles that clung to my beard. When I was thirsty, I'd suck them. The scariest was scuba diving with wild Nile crocodiles, in Botswana. One attacked our cameraman. He was only saved when

he stuck the camera in its mouth! The hardest was rowing across the Atlantic. It took 49 long, sleepless days. I was broken.

What advice would you give to a young person with a love of the outdoors and travel?
Enjoy it. Be curious. Respect the weather and the wilderness but don't be afraid of it; work with the weather and the wilderness like they're a part of your team. Too many think it's a battle against the wild – it isn't. It's a beautiful friendship.

Books set in far-flung places

Escape into strange new lands with these gripping page-turners.

From the Amazon rainforest to the wilds of Australia and the peaks of the Himalayan mountains, stories can take us on journeys around the world. Words on a page have the power to whisk you from the sofa in your sitting room to places you'd normally need a passport to explore. The best books will leave you feeling as though you've actually been elsewhere – the sights, the sounds and the smells will come alive in your imagination. There are many wonderful stories set in countries far from home; here are five that are guaranteed to whet your appetite for international adventures…

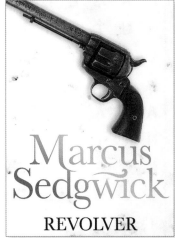

Revolver
by Marcus Sedgwick

(Hachette Children's Group)

It's 1910, and in a cabin in the snowy wilderness, north of the Arctic Circle, 14-year-old Sig is all by himself. That's until a sinister man turns up. Who is he, and what does he want? Sig soon realises he may be in danger. This award-winning thriller is set against bleak snowy landscapes that match its atmosphere of tension and fear.

The Island at the End of Everything
by Kiran Millwood Hargrave

(Chicken House)

Ami lives on an island in the Philippines, which is home to a community of people who have a disease called leprosy – among them Ami's beloved mother. However, when Mr Zamora arrives, their peaceful life is disturbed and Ami is torn from the home she loves.

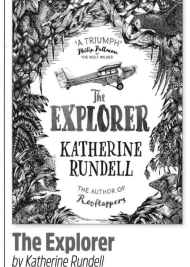

The Explorer
by Katherine Rundell

(Bloomsbury Publishing)

When their plane crashes in the Amazon jungle, Fred and three other children find themselves alone, stranded hundreds of miles from civilisation. In a strange new environment, with poisonous snakes and forest fires, they must try to find their way back home. This is a captivating story of adventure, friendship and bravery.

The Secret of Supernatural Creek
by Lauren St John

(Hachette Children's Group)

Eleven-year-old detective Laura Marlin's adventures have already taken her around the world. In the latest book in the series, Laura expects her holiday in Australia to be an ordinary school trip, but as she travels into the wilderness, there is mystery and danger in store.

Dragon Rider
by Cornelia Funke

(Chicken House)

Firedrake the silver dragon and his friends Ben and Sorrel set out on a daring mission to discover the mysterious Rim of Heaven, which is located somewhere high in the Himalayas. This bestselling adventure, from the author of *Inkheart,* is very much a fantasy tale, full of fabulous creatures and extraordinary magic, but the wonderful landscapes of the story are inspired by the real-life Himalayan mountains.

Wordsearch

Can you find all of these capital cities in the grid? They may be hidden horizontally, vertically or diagonally, and reading either forwards or backwards.

ABU DHABI
ALGIERS
ATHENS
BAGHDAD
BANGKOK
BEIJING
BELGRADE
BERLIN
BRIDGETOWN
BUCHAREST
BUDAPEST
CAIRO
CANBERRA
CARACAS
COPENHAGEN
DAMASCUS
HARARE
HELSINKI
JAKARTA
LISBON

LONDON
MADRID
MANILA
MONTEVIDEO
NAIROBI
NASSAU
PANAMA CITY
PORT OF SPAIN
PORT-AU-PRINCE
PRAGUE
REYKJAVIK
ROME
SAN SALVADOR
STOCKHOLM
TALLINN
TOKYO
VALLETTA
VIENNA
WARSAW
WELLINGTON

W	K	R	O	B	E	R	L	I	N	O	D	N	O	L	H	U	C	A	I
D	B	G	K	N	R	U	E	C	N	I	R	P	U	A	T	R	O	P	B
F	A	S	I	O	A	V	L	M	O	N	T	E	V	I	D	E	O	Z	B
F	G	M	V	B	R	S	A	B	N	C	O	S	A	C	A	R	A	C	U
U	H	F	A	I	A	S	S	L	K	O	U	T	M	T	T	O	S	K	D
N	D	A	J	S	H	H	B	A	L	P	B	D	G	O	D	D	I	C	A
R	A	I	K	Y	C	E	D	U	U	E	T	S	F	N	S	A	L	Z	P
D	D	U	Y	N	I	U	M	U	S	N	T	S	I	S	I	V	I	A	E
B	R	M	E	N	Z	O	S	O	B	H	P	T	I	L	M	L	N	T	S
A	U	T	R	I	B	E	L	G	R	A	D	E	A	W	M	A	L	B	T
E	Z	C	T	L	U	A	A	X	I	G	Y	Q	R	L	M	S	A	E	H
P	K	C	H	L	A	L	T	N	D	E	D	N	O	A	N	N	A	E	W
A	H	A	U	A	R	G	H	O	G	N	L	H	C	B	G	A	L	N	V
N	T	I	K	T	R	I	E	Y	E	P	K	I	E	K	E	S	I	A	D
N	Q	R	M	S	E	E	N	K	T	C	T	I	O	U	I	E	N	Q	L
E	C	O	A	U	B	R	S	O	O	Y	J	K	H	N	G	J	A	U	Q
I	M	A	D	K	N	S	X	T	W	I	Q	D	K	O	S	A	M	R	S
V	W	A	R	S	A	W	S	G	N	N	A	I	R	O	B	I	R	T	P
C	I	A	I	W	C	J	A	G	U	K	O	R	K	R	L	O	U	P	U
S	O	T	D	P	J	F	H	R	T	C	V	Y	O	B	E	G	Y	P	E

Sudoku

Place the numbers from 1-9 exactly once in each row, column and 3x3 bold-lined box to complete the grid.

2	5		1		7		4	9
	1	3	2		4	8	7	
				8				
		4	5	9				
1		4				5		3
		3	1	2				
				2				
	4	2	5		3	9	1	
8	6		7		1		5	2

Code riddles

Each of these US states has had each letter replaced by the letter after it in the alphabet (so A becomes B, B becomes C and so on). Can you break the code to reveal the answers?

DBMJGPSOJB =

OFX ZPSL =

GMPSJEB =

Number tower

Place a number in every square to complete the number tower. The value in each square is the sum of the numbers in the two squares directly beneath it.

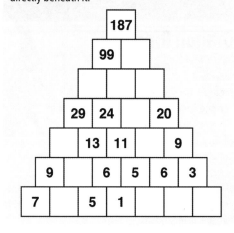

Number cross

All the numbers below appear exactly once in the puzzle grid. Can you work out where each one goes? We've placed one number to start you off.

4 numbers	7 numbers
2328	1139776
5518	4545380
5778	4812070
6186	9540852
6218	
9448	**8 numbers**
	27628089
5 numbers	64084958
49177	74243825
72798	86765255
75568	90892263
99486	91059628

6 numbers
~~342501~~
524661
821897
996676

ANSWERS CAN BE FOUND ON PAGES 94–97

Grid starting numbers (top-left): 3, 4, 2, 5, 0, 1

Keyword crossword

Once you have completed the crossword, use the letters in the highlighted boxes to form a word. Write it in the space below the clues.

Across
1. Time when the whole school gets together (8)
6. The joints between the thighs and the lower legs (5)
7. Something you sit on (5)
9. Story (4)
10. Knitted garment (6)
12. Sausage in a roll (3,3)
14. Enter a telephone number (4)
17. Edible fruits with hard stones (5)
18. Sweet on a stick (5)
19. House without an upstairs (8)

Down
2. Take illegally (5)
3. Compass point (4)
4. Water container (6)
5. 2018 and 2019, for instance (5)
6. Tomato sauce (7)
8. People such as the Queen and Prince Charles (7)
11. Child of your aunt or uncle (6)
13. You have one on each hand (5)
15. A house made from ice (5)
16. Tiny insect (4)

Keyword clue: A country bordering Austria

Anagrams

Rearrange the scrambled letters to spell out the names of three countries.

RENTAGAIN
(CLUE: A country in South America)

REDNAIL
(CLUE: The capital of this country is Dublin)

BIGMULE
(CLUE: You'll find this small country in Europe)

Spot the difference

Can you find five differences between these pictures?

HOW TO...
Make a travel journal
Hold on to your holiday memories.

Time flies by and it can be tricky trying to remember all of the adventures you've had. To help remind you of the places you've visited, try making a travel journal.

What you'll need
- Printed photos
- Holiday mementos, such as tickets, postcards and leaflets
- A scrapbook or a ring binder and paper
- Sticky tape
- Glue
- Coloured pens
- Stickers (optional)

Instructions
1. First, gather together all of the pictures and mementos you want to include in your journal.
2. Arrange them in chronological order, which means the order in which they happened.
3. Take your book or binder and lay out your first page.
4. Once you've stuck the photos and/or mementos down, write around them what you did there and any fun things you'd like to remember.
5. You can also use stickers and different coloured pens to decorate the page.
6. Repeat until your journal is filled with fantastic memories.

HANDY HINT
When you're out and about, pick up leaflets and maps so that you can cut bits out to stick on your pages. Take a ziplock bag with you on your travels to keep your mementos safe.

PERFECT POCKETS
To keep smaller souvenirs, such as tickets, stamps or even sweet wrappers safe inside your journal, stick an envelope to the page and pop them inside.

MAP IT OUT
Why not print maps of where you've been? You could stick a map in the middle of a page and circle exactly where you were, before sticking your mementos around it.

WRAP IT UP
Wrap string, ribbon or an elastic band vertically around your journal to keep the contents together.

MAKING MEMORIES
When you're on holiday, carry a small notepad around with you so that you can jot down the sights, sounds and smells you experience. Your notes will make it easier to recall the memories when you put your journal together.

KEEP COINS
Put unspent foreign coins inside a ziplock bag and stick it in your journal to remind you of that country's currency.

SNAPPING SIGNS
Take pictures of any signs you see including the roads you travel on, the hotels you stay at or the restaurants you visit. You can then print them out and pop them in your journal.

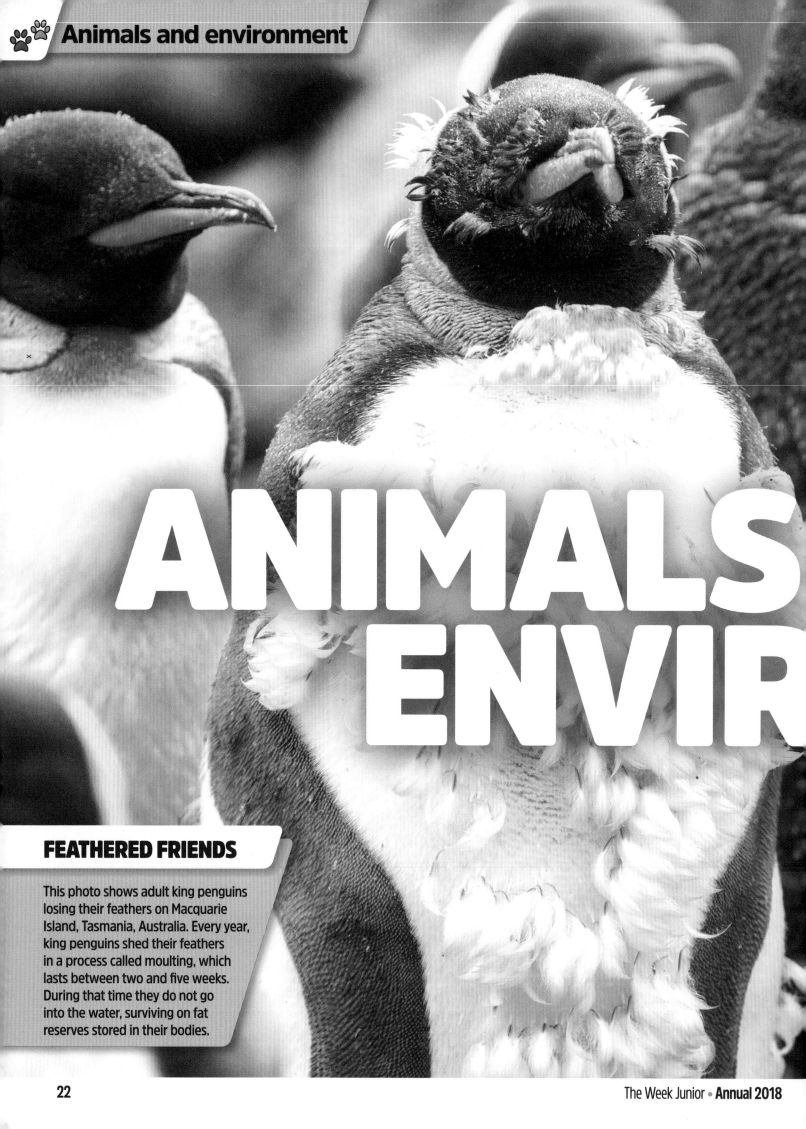

ANIMALS
ENVIR

FEATHERED FRIENDS

This photo shows adult king penguins losing their feathers on Macquarie Island, Tasmania, Australia. Every year, king penguins shed their feathers in a process called moulting, which lasts between two and five weeks. During that time they do not go into the water, surviving on fat reserves stored in their bodies.

AND
ONMENT

Meet some strange and wonderful creatures and discover what you can do to protect our planet.

Protecting our planet

From bags to bottles, plastic is choking the world. But what is it, and how can we clean it up?

In 2017, scientists calculated that humans had produced around 8.3 billion tonnes of plastic over the last 65 years. That is heavier than a billion elephants.

Most plastic is non-biodegradable, which means that it can't break down naturally. A lot of the plastic that is thrown away ends up in a landfill (land where rubbish is dumped or buried). Experts estimate that there is enough plastic on the planet right now to cover an area more than 10 times the size of the UK.

Plastic has disastrous consequences for the planet. It pollutes our oceans and causes animals to become sick. Scientists and conservationists are trying to come up with new ways to reduce the amount of plastic on Earth.

DID YOU KNOW?
The word plastic comes from the Greek word *plastikos*, which means to shape or form.

What is plastic?

Plastic is the general term for a wide range of synthetic materials. Synthetic means artificially created by combining chemicals. Plastic can be moulded into different shapes, and lots of things are made from it, such as bags, bottles and toys. Even some materials for making clothes contain plastic fibres.

The first fully synthetic plastic was developed by Leo Hendrik Baekeland in 1907. It changed the way people lived. Nearly every industry was affected by the invention of plastic and it suddenly became far cheaper to make things from plastic than it was to use natural materials like wood or glass. One of the first items to be made from plastic was the comb; before plastic, combs were often made from animal bone or horn. Another item that changed dramatically was the milk bottle. Compared with traditional glass bottles, plastic cartons can be manufactured much more cheaply and quickly. They are also a great deal lighter and less breakable than glass.

How does plastic affect our environment?

STRUGGLING MARINE LIFE

There are an estimated 245,000 tonnes of plastic floating in our oceans. According to a study by researchers at Plymouth University, this floating plastic debris has affected around 700 species of marine life. Small pieces of plastic get mixed up in marine algae (a type of sea plant) and fish end up eating it, which can harm them.

OVERFLOWING LANDFILL SITES

Around 1.5 million tonnes of recyclable plastic is thrown away by British households every year, and around two thirds of this is sent to landfill. Plastics decompose at different rates; bottles can take up to around 450 years to break down naturally, and landfill sites cannot cope with the amount that people are throwing away.

rom plastic

PLASTIC POLLUTION
UK households fail to recycle around 16 million plastic bottles every day.

It takes a long time for plastic to break down.

Plastic is a huge problem in the world, but there are things you can do to help. Here are a few top tips to help you avoid being part of the problem.

BUY A BAG FOR LIFE

A bag for life is a bag you can use over and over again. Single-use plastic bags are polluting our oceans. Turtles often mistake the floating bags for jellyfish and try to eat them.

STOP BUYING BOTTLED WATER

Instead of buying bottled water, ask your parents to get you a reusable stainless steel bottle that can be refilled as many times as you like.

STOP USING STRAWS

Plastic straws might be fun to blow bubbles in your drink, but they are really bad for the environment. Try using reusable metal or glass straws instead.

Microbeads are found in many toiletries.

POLAR REGIONS

Scientists have revealed that plastic dumped in the oceans around the UK is travelling to the Arctic within two years. Trillions of pieces of this plastic are getting trapped in Arctic ice. If the Arctic ice melts, all of the plastic will be released from the ice and fall back into the ocean, where it will harm more marine life.

TOXIC AIR

Plastics are made from petroleum or natural gas. Destroying plastics releases toxic chemicals into the air and pollutes the atmosphere.

BANNED MICROBEADS
Microbeads are tiny plastic balls found in toiletries such as face wash and toothpaste, which end up in our oceans. The UK Government will ban them in June 2018.

Not amused
This Dalmatian pelican in Greece glares at the photographer.

Star seeds
An up-close picture of a star of Persia plant.

Peek-a-boo
A pink skunk clownfish peeks out from a sea anemone in Thailand.

PROTECTING PLANET EARTH
Greenpeace is a charity that helps protect the planet. It was founded in 1971 by a small group of people and now works in more than 40 countries all over the world.

ARCTIC SUNRISE

Bon voyage
A Greenpeace mission to Bear Island, which lies between Norway and the North Pole.

Going dotty
Newly laid frogspawn looks like lots of little eyes.

WARNING SPOTS
Despite what some people might say, you can't tell the age of a ladybird by counting its spots. The spots are there to scare off predators.

On a roll
A zebra rolls around in the sand in Etosha National Park in Namibia.

Soggy slither
A Madagascar water snake goes for a swim.

Take a break
A ladybird rests on an oriental poppy flower.

WILL ROSE/GREENPEACE

STRANGE AND SURPRISING
ANIMALS

These crafty creatures have a few sneaky tricks up their sleeves...

Our planet is home to millions of amazingly adapted animals. From those that roam the land to birds that soar across the skies, and the peculiar creatures that live in the very depths of the oceans, Earth is teeming with life. Some are particularly strange-looking; others are equipped with ingenious special skills allowing them to keep cool, protect their young or defend themselves against predators. Here are just a few of Earth's most fantastic beasts – and where to find them.

CRAZY CLIMBER
The Hispaniolan solenodon is able to climb almost vertical surfaces.

Hispaniolan solenodon

This mammal has an unusually long, flexible snout, which it uses to sniff out prey in cracks on the forest floor.

- **HABITAT:** Hispaniolan solenodons can only be found living in forests on Hispaniola, the second-largest island in the Caribbean.

- **LIFESPAN IN THE WILD:** Up to 11 years.

- **DIET:** Mostly invertebrates such as crickets, earthworms and termites, but it has also been known to eat amphibians, small birds and reptiles.

- **FUN FACT:** These mammals produce toxic saliva, which they use to paralyse their prey.

Great hornbill

The first thing many people notice about the great hornbill is its impressive horn, called a casque, which sits on its head and beak. This unusual addition makes its calls louder. The casque is also used by males to fight for females.

- **HABITAT:** The evergreen forests of Asia, from Sumatra to India.

- **LIFESPAN IN THE WILD:** 35–40 years.

- **DIET:** The great hornbill feeds mainly on fruit but will also snack on amphibians, birds, insects and small mammals.

- **FUN FACT:** The iris (the ring around the pupil in the eye) of the male great hornbill is red; the female's irises are white.

DID YOU KNOW?
When a female great hornbill finds a suitable hole in a tree to nest, she uses her and her partner's poo to block the entrance, trapping her inside with her eggs. She makes a small gap in the newly built poo wall for her partner to pass through food.

Saltwater crocodile

ROCKY LUNCH
These reptiles swallow stones and pebbles to help grind the food in their stomachs.

At around five to seven metres long, the saltwater croc is the largest reptile in the world. It is unusual for many reasons, not least that it can replace all its teeth lots of times during its life.

- **HABITAT:** Found in coastal waters, rivers and mangrove forests from Sri Lanka, across Southeast Asia to Australia.

- **LIFESPAN IN THE WILD:** Around 70 years.

- **DIET:** The saltwater croc eats lots of things, including cattle, fish and wallabies.

- **FUN FACT:** It is often spotted lying on river banks with its jaws wide open. It does this because it cools down through its mouth, a bit like panting.

BIZARRE BIRTHING
The female Surinam toad carries fertilised eggs in the skin on her back. It is here that they develop into tiny toadlets, before erupting out of her back.

Bombardier beetle

Growing up to 2.5 centimetres long, the bombardier beetle has a unique – and effective – method of defending itself. When under threat from an attacker, it fires a very hot mixture of poisonous chemicals – from its backside!

- **HABITAT:** Woodlands and grasslands on every continent except Antarctica.

- **LIFESPAN IN THE WILD:** Several weeks.

- **DIET:** The bombardier beetle eats during the night, feasting on smaller insects.

- **FUN FACT:** Although it has wings, the beetle is not good at flying.

Leafy sea dragon

With its stretched-out snout and bony-plated body, this unusual-looking sea creature is related to species such as seahorses and pipefish.

- **HABITAT:** Amid seaweed in the shallow coastal waters of south and east Australia.

- **LIFESPAN IN THE WILD:** Thought to be up to seven years.

- **DIET:** Small organisms, including mysids (small, shrimp-like creatures) and plankton.

- **FUN FACT:** Male leafy sea dragons carry the eggs of their young in a pouch, where they hatch.

Surinam toad

These amphibians never sit up on their front limbs like other types of toad. The Surinam toad has an unusual flat body.

- **HABITAT:** Muddy rivers, streams and pools in South American rainforests.

- **LIFESPAN IN THE WILD:** Up to 10 years, though possibly longer.

- **DIET:** Small fish and vertebrates, which Surinam toads detect through star-shaped sensors on the ends of their fingers.

- **FUN FACT:** The Surinam toad does not have a tongue. Instead it has to use its long fingers to scoop prey into its mouth.

The bionic vet

England's top vet treats animals like humans.

Deep in the heart of the countryside is one of the most extraordinary veterinary practices in the UK: Fitzpatrick Referrals. Owned by Noel Fitzpatrick, also known as the bionic vet, the practice treats some of the sickest animals in the country. Fitzpatrick's philosophy is to treat animals the same as you would humans. He has given animals who can't walk bionic (artificial) limbs and has treated inoperable spine injuries. His cutting-edge treatment, using the latest technology, has made him the star of the Channel 4 TV show *Supervet* for the last three years.

Born in Laois in Ireland, Fitzpatrick credits his love of animals to his childhood dog, Pirate, who was his best friend growing up. When he was little, Fitzpatrick had trouble reading and writing, and as a result he was bullied at his school. He says that Pirate helped him get through his childhood because the dog was always there for him. Despite his troubles, Fitzpatrick went on to study veterinary medicine at University College Dublin.

He opened Fitzpatrick Referrals in 2005, but it isn't like any normal veterinary practice. Instead of cages, there are glass doors with huge rooms where animals can roam free. Animals are also given comfy air beds, blankets, TV and radio. He doesn't just treat pets; he is also a big fan of treating wild animals. "Hedgehogs are my favourite," he says. Although Fitzpatrick has already done a lot for animals that have been deemed untreatable by other vets, he doesn't want to stop there. In 2014, he started a charity called Humanimal Trust. The charity aims to create one approach to medicine for animals and humans alike. "It frustrated me that animals were used to develop modern medical care but human medicine never came back to help animals," he says. "I strongly wish that there should only be one medicine."

24-HOUR CARE
Fitzpatrick is so passionate about the animals he treats, he sleeps in his surgery.

Noel Fitzpatrick is also known as the bionic vet.

HARD WORK
Since he set up Fitzpatrick Referrals, Fitzpatrick hasn't taken a holiday for 14 years.

INTERVIEW

Noel Fitzpatrick

The bionic vets tells *The Week Junior* which animal(s) he would most like to be.

What are the best and worst parts of your job?
When animals come to me in pain and in need and we are able to successfully care for them and give them a new quality of life – that means the world to me. The worst part of the job is when we try to do all we possibly can for an animal, but end up losing the battle and the animal loses its life.

What made you want to advance technology to help sick animals?
I was very frustrated by the lack of options available for my patients, and I realised that I could either spend my career feeling powerless, or I could do something to make a real difference. It is very important that we embrace the technological revolution in medicine.

If you had an animal alter ego, what would it be?
I'd be a kind of chimera – which is a fusion of a few animals. I'd like to be strong like a rhinoceros; agile like a gazelle; able to see behind me like an owl; have really good day and night vision like a leopard; be a speedy swimmer like a sailfish; live long like a tortoise; be flexible like a sea lion, and I'd really like to be able to fly!

Do you have any pets?
I have a lovely border terrier called Keira. She comes to work every day and I spend weekends with her. We go on adventures and create mayhem.

What advice would you give?
Believe in yourself and work very hard. Nobody has the right to rob you of your dream, so never let anybody tell you it is impossible.

Books narrated by animals

Burrow your way into the heart of the animal kingdom with these wild reads.

What would your cat say if it could talk? How about a dog, a horse or even a hamster? Writers have long been fascinated with telling stories in animals' voices; think of *The Call of the Wild* and *Black Beauty*, both of which were written more than 100 years ago. Tales like these will take you on an adventure to the heart of the animal kingdom and make you see the world differently. The animal narrators of these five fantastic books – whether a lonely urban fox, a courageous rabbit or a cat with special powers – each tell a story from their own point of view and in their own, distinctive voice.

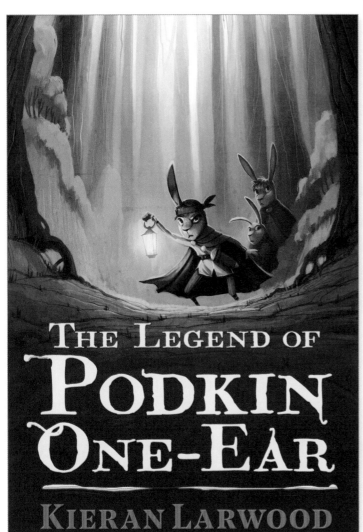

The Legend of Podkin One-Ear
by Kieran Larwood. Illustrated by David Wyatt

(Faber Children's Books)

Podkin is the young son of a rabbit warrior chieftain. When his warren is brutally attacked by a dark power known as the Gorm, his family are forced to run for their lives. Can Podkin follow in his father's footsteps by protecting his family and taking a stand against the terrible enemy that threatens rabbitkind? A thrilling story with a fantastic hero in Podkin, it's no surprise this book scooped the Blue Peter Book Award 2017.

Pax
by Sara Pennypacker.
Illustrated by Jon Klassen

(HarperCollins Children's Books)

Peter rescues a baby fox and rears it as a pet – but when his dad enlists in the military, he is forced to release it back into the wild. Told in alternating chapters from the perspectives of Peter and Pax the fox, this is the beautifully written story of how the two friends try to find their way back to each other.

Toto
by Michael Morpurgo.
Illustrated by Emma Chichester Clark

(HarperCollins Children's Books)

Michael Morpurgo's book is a fun new spin on *The Wizard of Oz*. Here, the much-loved adventures of Dorothy, Cowardly Lion, Scarecrow and Tin Man are retold from the point of view of Dorothy's dog, Toto. Gorgeously illustrated in bright colours, this is an exciting new version of a popular classic.

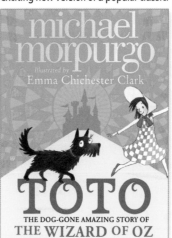

The River Singers
by Tom Moorhouse.
Illustrated by Simon Mendez

(Oxford University Press)

The River Singers are a family of water voles, living peacefully on the banks of the Great River. However, when danger threatens, young vole Sylvan and his brother and sisters must leave their sheltered burrow behind. This is the story of their journey to find a safe new home.

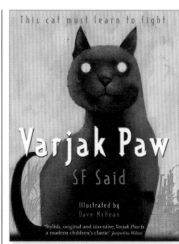

Varjak Paw
by S.F. Said.
Illustrated by Dave McKean

(Random House Children's Books)

This is the story of Varjak Paw – a rare, Mesopotamian Blue kitten who's never been outside. When the sinister Gentleman takes over his home, Varjak must venture out for help. Can his mystical ancestor, Jalal, and the ancient Way – a secret martial art for cats – help him survive the dangers of the city?

Wordsearch

ANSWERS CAN BE FOUND ON PAGES 94–97

Can you find all of these animals in the grid? Words may be hidden horizontally, vertically or diagonally, and reading either forwards or backwards.

ANTELOPE
ARMADILLO
BABOON
BADGER
BEAVER
BUFFALO
CAMEL
CHAMELEON
CHEETAH
CHICKEN
CHIMPANZEE
CHIPMUNK
CROCODILE
DINGO
DOLPHIN
DONKEY
ELEPHANT
FERRET
FLAMINGO
GAZELLE

GECKO
GERBIL
GIBBON
GIRAFFE
GUINEA PIG
HAMSTER
HEDGEHOG
HIPPOPOTAMUS
HORSE
KANGAROO
LEOPARD
MONGOOSE
PANDA
POLAR BEAR
PORCUPINE
REINDEER
RHINOCEROS
TORTOISE
WHALE
WOLF

```
M N S G X N M G E C K O L I A E T L S H
D O P L E O P A R D C L P I D U V E A X
N B A D G E R C R T H A O G N I D A B C
T B D V H L H L A O I F N R A S T H A S
A I W E N E I P R H P F K T P Z E M P L
S G L U E M E S K N M U O N E D E O K I
U I Q T K A E T O T U B T G G L R L C B
M L A V C H I M P A N Z E E E C O M L R
A H V C I C K V Y O K S H P U C G P R E
T Q I I H X K S W Q L O H P G L N O E G
O L L E C L A G O K G A I A U T I I I L
P C E S F K N D L R N N R P I S M D N B
O B E I J F G B F T E M S B N H A P D F
P U E O B E A V E R A C D H E N L V E W
P N G T R B R R F D T W O O A A F W E N
I I C R O C O D I L E H N N P M R O R L
H T T O U S O L V G G A K L I A S D X P
T D N T D O L P H I N L E G G H X T N P
A P F Z M O N G O O S E Y C F E R R E T
E O J A A Q Y P S Y C A G J K A A T O R
```

Sudoku

Place each number from 1–9 exactly once in each row, column and bold-lined 3x3 box. Can you complete the grid and solve the sudoku puzzle?

8	2		5		6		9	4
6		5		2		1		3
	9	4	1		8	6	2	
	5		4		1		6	
1		9				5		2
	4		2		5		3	
	3	7	8		2	4	5	
4		2		5		3		8
5	8		3		7		1	9

Code riddles

Each of these animal homes has had each letter replaced by the letter after it in the alphabet (so A becomes B, B becomes C and so on). Can you break the code to reveal the answers?

IVUDI =

TUBCMF =

CFFIJWF =

Number tower

Place a number in every square to complete the number tower. The value in each square is the sum of the numbers in the two squares directly beneath it.

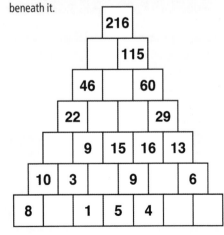

```
            216
              115
         46      60
      22            29
         9   15  16  13
      10  3       9      6
   8       1   5   4
```

The Week Junior • **Annual 2018**

Number cross

All the numbers below appear exactly once in the puzzle grid. Can you work out where each one goes? We've placed one number to start you off.

3 numbers
180
573

4 numbers
5476
9255

5 numbers
12247
17615
18270
27510
53244
54500
56734
77971

6 numbers
206896
241197

7 numbers
1055291
1222910
3375578
4454286

8 numbers
82808376
~~92391151~~

12 numbers
726619147008
931475106253

13 numbers
1276156331146
9947113554278

Grid entry: 9 2 3 9 1 1 5 1

Anagrams

Rearrange the scrambled letters to form the names of birds.

CHECKIN
(CLUE: Widely eaten around the world)

APENCIL
(CLUE: These birds have long beaks)

ONEPIG
(CLUE: You'll see lots of these in big cities)

Keyword crossword

Once you have completed the crossword, use the letters in the highlighted boxes to form a word. Write it in the space below the clues.

Across
1. For example, the use of the imagination (10)
5. Cyclist (5)
7. Perfect role model (5)
9. Raised up (6)
10. Opposite of right (4)
12. Bite and munch food (4)
13. Continent (6)
16. You need this to make a sandwich (5)
17. Choose a politician for office (5)
18. Tasty red fruit (10)

Down
1. Christmas song (5)
2. Aim (6)
3. Blood vessel (4)
4. As a result; so (9)
6. Not the same (9)
8. Allow to happen (3)
11. Wonderful (6)
12. A young bear or lion (3)
14. Way into a place (5)
15. Suggestion (4)

Keyword clue: Using again

Spot the difference

Can you find the five differences between these pictures?

HOW TO...
Reduce your carbon footprint

There are lots of ways to make the planet a greener place.

Your carbon footprint is a measure of how much your daily life affects the environment. We all have one, even if we can't see it. It's all the greenhouse gases, such as carbon dioxide, that you, individually, cause to be produced in your day-to-day activities. Greenhouse gases contribute to global warming and are mainly a result of burning fossil fuels. The way you travel, the electricity you use, even the food you eat and the clothes you buy can add to your carbon footprint. There are choices you can make that will reduce the impact you have on the planet, and help protect it for the future. Here are a few ways you can make a difference.

WOW! Globally, 27,000 trees' worth of toilet paper is flushed every day.

Eat less meat

Did you know that the production of meat is the biggest contributor to the world's emissions of methane? Methane is a far more powerful greenhouse gas than carbon dioxide, and contributes heavily to global warming. Reducing the amount of meat you eat is a really good way to help the planet. There are lots of tasty vegetarian recipes to try, and many are fun and simple to prepare. Why not ask an adult to help you whip up a delicious curry? Take a look here: tinyurl.com/twj-recipe

Make your own gifts

There are lots of fun ways to care for the environment, some of which you might not have considered. For example, wrapping gifts doesn't have to cost the Earth. Why not have a rummage and see if there's something lying around the house you could recycle instead of buying wrapping paper? Brown paper bags, old calendars, newspapers, magazines and old boxes can all be used to make your gifts look gorgeous and unique, especially if you add some ribbon, stickers, string and some of your own artwork. You could even make your own presents – you can't beat homemade biscuits in a nicely decorated jar, tin or box.

Get everyone involved

The more people who know about the simple things we can do to protect the planet, the better. Perhaps you could get together with friends and organise an assembly about climate change at school, with some tips for how to make your school greener, or hold a cake sale to raise money for your favourite animal-conservation charity. You could even talk to your teachers about organising a sponsored walk-to-school week. In 2018 the event will be held on 14 –18 May.

What do you do to help protect the planet?
Write some of your own ideas or goals in the space below.

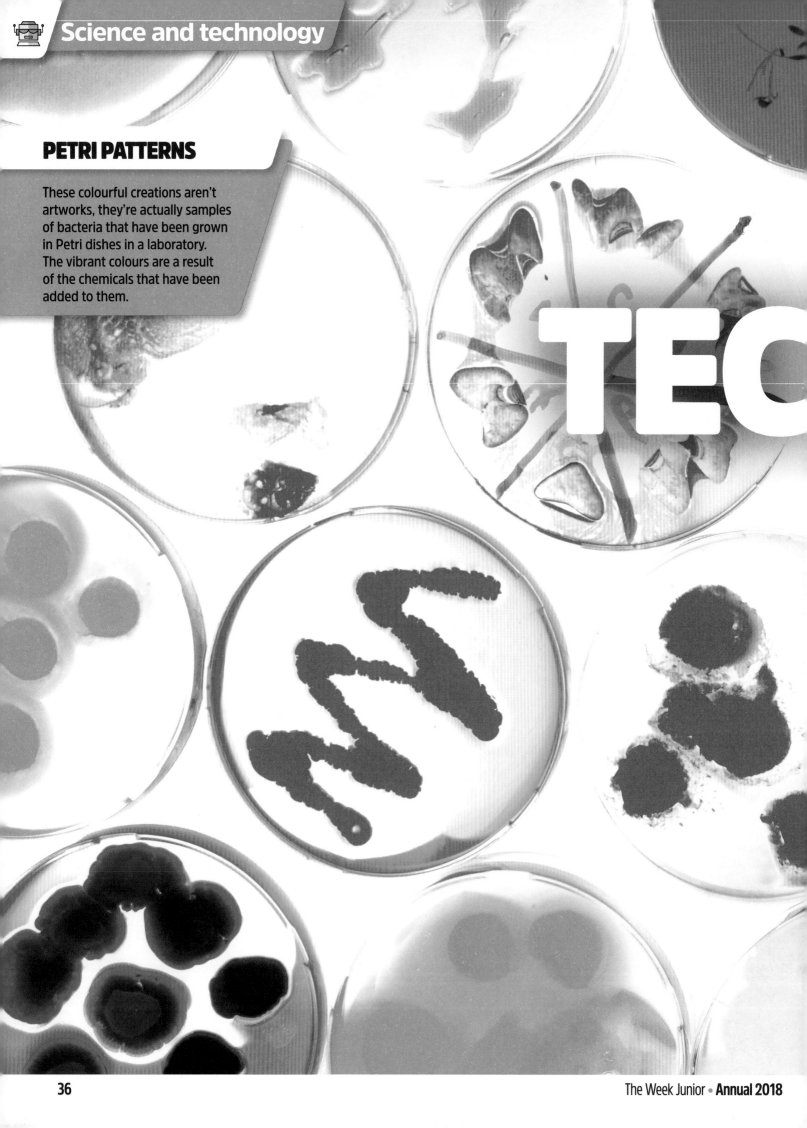

PETRI PATTERNS

These colourful creations aren't artworks, they're actually samples of bacteria that have been grown in Petri dishes in a laboratory. The vibrant colours are a result of the chemicals that have been added to them.

TEC

SCIENCE &
TECHNOLOGY

If you've ever wondered how flight works, what worlds there might be beyond Earth or what you can do to brush up your own scientific skills... read on.

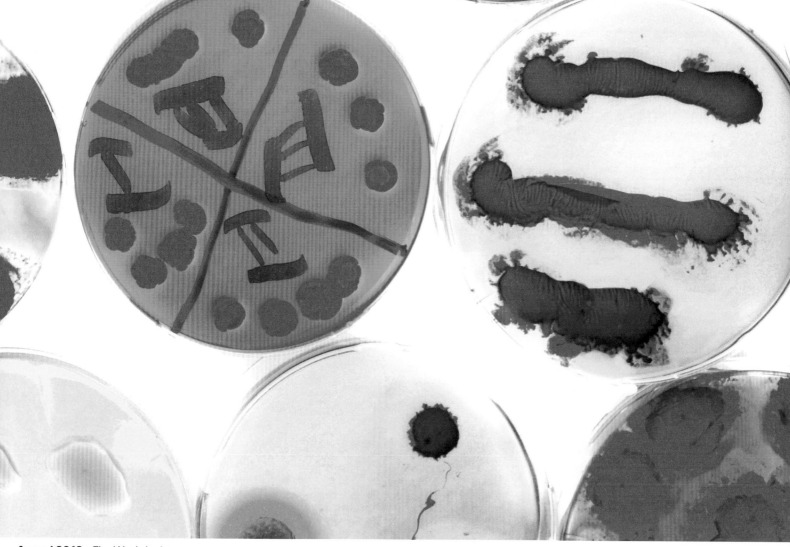

The fabulous history

It took a long time for the dream of flying to become reality.

Humans are heavy and not designed for flight; we lack the powerful chest muscles and hollow bones that birds use for flapping flight. Many early attempts to fly like a birdman – using wings made from lightweight wood or feathers – ended in disaster. Finally, people took to the skies in hot-air balloons. Even today, these flying machines are not much more than a basket slung underneath a huge bag filled with warm air.

The Wright brothers made the first engine-powered flight at the start of the 20th century and ever since, inventions have come thick and fast. Just 44 years after that maiden flight, humans were travelling faster than the speed of sound. The Flyer – as the brothers' flying machine was known – was essentially a powered glider, and could only carry the pilot. Its first flight was less than the distance between a jumbo jet's wingtips. Today's largest passenger jet, by contrast, is longer than two blue whales, can carry 525 people, with space for 3,000 suitcases, and can fly about 9,000 miles on one tank of fuel.

WOW! There are more Boeing 737s than any other jetliner. More than 9,600 of them have been built since the 737's first flight, on 9 April 1967.

We have lift-off!

Hot-air balloons work by flotation, where the large volume of warm air in the balloon is less dense and therefore lighter than the air outside the balloon. However, to get something heavier than air off the ground requires a lifting force that acts against gravity. This is where the special shape of a wing comes in. As air flows over a wing, its "aerofoil" shape creates high air pressure on the bottom surface and lower pressure on the upper surface. If the air is travelling fast enough, the pressure difference will generate enough force to lift an aircraft into the air. The larger the wing's surface area, the greater the lift.

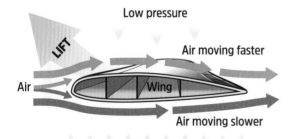

Low pressure

LIFT

Air moving faster

Air — Wing

Air moving slower

High pressure

The sky is the limit: Air-travel timeline

1783
FIRST BALLOON FLIGHT
French brothers, Joseph-Michel and Jacques-Etienne Montgolfier, design the first passenger hot-air balloon.

1903
FIRST SUCCESSFUL AEROPLANE
On 17 December 1903, Orville and Wilbur Wright pilot The Flyer on four flights in North Carolina, US.

1927
FIRST SOLO FLIGHT ACROSS THE ATLANTIC OCEAN
Charles Lindbergh flies his single-engine plane, Spirit of St Louis, from New York and lands near Paris.

# of flying machines

FLYING ANIMALS

The Montgolfier brothers may have designed the first hot-air balloon for people, but for safety, the first passengers were a cockerel, sheep and a duck.

Pioneering pilot

Many early aviators were women. British pilot Amy Johnson earned her pilot's licence in 1929, and was soon breaking records. She was the first woman to fly solo from England to Australia, and set speed records with flights to Japan and South Africa. During the Second World War, Johnson delivered new military planes to air bases and flew them between airfields.

The future of flying?

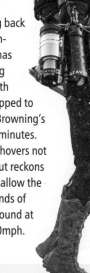

They call him the real-life Iron Man... British inventor Richard Browning is bringing back the era of the human-powered flight and has built the first working jet-powered suit. With six gas turbines strapped to his back and arms, Browning's flights last up to 12 minutes. For the moment, he hovers not far off the ground, but reckons his suit will one day allow the wearer to fly thousands of metres above the ground at speeds of nearly 300mph.

Pilots control a plane from the cockpit.

1947
SOUND BARRIER BROKEN

Test pilot Chuck Yeager flies a Bell X-1 rocket plane, nicknamed Glamorous Glennis, faster than the speed of sound.

SPEED OF SOUND

At 20°C in dry air, sound travels at about 343 metres per second, or 767mph.

1969
FIRST LANDING ON THE MOON

Massive Apollo rockets take Neil Armstrong, Buzz Aldrin and Mike Collins to the Moon.

2007
LARGEST PASSENGER PLANE LAUNCHED

The double-decker Airbus A380 carries more people and uses less fuel per passenger than other airliners.

NASA

WOW!
The space-travel company Virgin Galactic hopes that the Unity spacecraft will one day be used to carry tourists into space.

Flying high
The Virgin Galactic spacecraft, Unity, on a test flight in May 2017. It launched from the Mojave Air and Space Port in California, US.

3D gnome
A model of a gnome is scanned by a machine that can use the images to create a duplicate.

Space art
Artist Mik Petter created this colourful artwork using data from the JunoCam imager on board Nasa's Juno spacecraft.

NASA, VIRGIN GALACTIC

DID YOU KNOW?
In 1991, data captured by the Very Large Array contributed to the discovery of ice on the planet Mercury. Mercury is the closest planet to our Sun.

Hot stuff
This dramatic image is made up from several photos of magnetic particles swirling on the Sun's surface.

Scouring the skies
The Very Large Array is an observatory in New Mexico, US. It is made up of 27 radio antennae, each of which has a 25-metre-wide dish.

Mirror, mirror
Nasa's James Webb Space Telescope has 18 hexagonal gold-coated mirrors to see infrared light from the first galaxies to form in the early universe.

WEIRD WORLDS

The search for life on other worlds has led scientists to some brilliant discoveries.
Here are six of the most interesting planets that have been spotted so far.

A precious planet

Imagine a planet that is made from diamonds. Well, that's exactly what scientists think a planet called 55 Cancri e could be. It takes around 18 hours to orbit its sun, and its surface temperature is a scorching 2,150°C. The planet is thought to be mainly made up of carbon (a chemical element) and the extreme temperature creates the perfect conditions for diamonds to form. Diamonds are pure forms of carbon that have been squeezed in extreme pressure and heated to very high temperatures. 55 Cancri e is about 40 light years from Earth.

DID YOU KNOW?

One light year is a measurement equal to around six trillion miles – that's roughly the distance travelled by a beam of light in one year.

The Star Wars planet

If you're a fan of *Star Wars* then you might remember Tatooine – the planet where Luke Skywalker grew up. It had two suns and looked like a dry, desert world. In 2011, Nasa discovered a planet about 200 light years from Earth that orbits two suns. Unlike Tatooine, this planet is thought to be too cold to harbour any life. Named Kepler-16b, the planet is about the same size as Saturn – which means that around 764 Earths could fit inside it – and is made up of half rock and half gas.

HOTTEST PLANET

KELT-9b is a planet a bit like Jupiter but it has a surface temperature of more than 4,300°C. That's hotter than most stars, and makes it the hottest planet ever found.

42

PATTERNS IN THE SKY

A constellation is a group of stars that form a pattern. The constellation Cancer forms a shape a bit like a crab – cancer is the Latin word for crab.

The planet with a gassy tail

About 33 light years from Earth, in the constellation Leo, lies a comet-like planet called GJ 436b. The planet is about the size of Neptune (Neptune's diameter is almost four times that of Earth's), and has a stream of gas flowing behind it. The gas is mostly made up of hydrogen, and astronomers believe that it is more than nine million miles long. It is called a comet-like planet because comets also have a tail of gas when they orbit close to a sun.

The dark planet

Astronomers think they have found a planet so dark that it reflects hardly any light at all. TrES-2b is blacker than a lump of coal or the blackest paint. The planet's darkness has puzzled scientists since they found it in 2006. One explanation is that the planet is covered in light-absorbing chemicals, such as sodium and titanium oxide. The planet is not completely pitch black, though. It has a temperature of around 980°C, which gives the surface a slight tint of red, a bit like glowing embers in a dying fire.

The puffy planet

In 2006, astronomers discovered a planet that is so light that if there were a bathtub big enough, the planet would float in the water. HAT-P-1b is located around 450 light years away, in the constellation Lacerta. It is part of a collection of planets nicknamed "hot Jupiters". They earned their name because they are roughly the same size as Jupiter but much, much hotter because they orbit closer to their suns. Scientists think that something inside HAT-P-1b is heating up, causing the planet to puff up.

A watery world

Discovered in 2011, Kepler-22b is almost 600 light years from Earth and is around 2.4 times larger than our planet. Scientists think the planet could have water because it is located in the Goldilocks Zone – an area around a star that is not too hot and not too cold for liquid water to exist. The surface of the planet is a comfortable 22°C, and scientists are studying Kepler-22b for possible signs of life.

FASTEST PLANET

Kepler-78b is about 100 times closer to its star than the Earth is to the Sun. It zooms around its sun in just 8.5 hours, making it one of the fastest planets ever discovered.

Annual 2018 • The Week Junior   43

Out-of-this-world laughs

Dara O Briain combines science and comedy.

You'll probably recognise Dara O Briain as one of the hosts of hit BBC machine-battle extravaganza, *Robot Wars*. However, O Briain isn't only a television personality – he's also one of the UK and Ireland's favourite stand-up comedians, a writer and a self-described science geek.

When Dara O Briain was at school, he was quite quiet, with a deep interest in maths and physics. So how did he go on to become one of the funniest people of his generation?

O Briain grew up in Ireland, where he attended a school that taught in both English and Irish. He remembers school as an exciting place, where people enjoyed debating and discussing issues. It was there that he discovered his first love – not comedy, but physics. Thanks to a teacher who was unafraid to stray from the syllabus, and teach his pupils all about the universe's most exciting and mysterious phenomena, O Briain developed a passion for the subject.

He went on to study physics at university, and that's where he found the talent that was to make him a star: comedy. Back then, it didn't seem like a career option. "I didn't think I'd ever end up being a comedian," he remembers. "There's a lot more comics now, but at that time we were all going, 'Wow, is this actually a real job we can do for the rest of our lives?'"

O Briain's first taste of television success wasn't as a comedian; his breakout role was as a children's TV presenter. His ability to speak both English and Irish came in useful when he hosted the Irish children's TV show *Echo Island*, which was presented in both languages.

He's the perfect fit for *Robot Wars*, in which top-level engineering results in thrilling fights between robots. He's also returning to his first love, physics, presenting *Stargazing Live*, a special live show in which he teams up with celebrity scientist, Brian Cox, to stare into the cosmos.

Now, he's written a children's book, *Beyond the Sky*, which combines his science knowledge and trademark wit. He's brought his two passions together into one job – but which does he prefer? "Comedy just tips science," he says. Luckily, he doesn't have to choose between them.

Q&A

Dara O Briain

The science-loving comic talks robots, relativity and reading.

Were you the funniest person at school in your class?
Not at all. In fact, I don't remember particularly being a clown at school. It only came to me when I'd already left school. Surprisingly few class clowns become comedians – they end up being the funniest guy among your mates at five-a-side football.

If you built a *Robot Wars* robot, what would its weapon be?
The *Robot Wars* arms race constantly bounces between flippers and spinners, so I would have to unleash something that would be neither flipper nor spinner. Sadly, I can't work out what that would be at the moment – nor can anyone else. Maybe it would lift up on its giant legs and then just sit on other robots.

What inspired your interest in physics?
When I was about 12 I had a teacher who taught us about black holes, and space, and relativity and these things. I was just at the right age to go, "Wow". And then I really got into it, I started reading loads of books about it and getting loads of popular science books. It was just because at a right age somebody told me a couple of great facts about black holes.

What would you say to someone who loves physics but finds maths really hard?
The people who are really good at maths, like I was, aren't always any good at building things. So even if you're not a numbers person, you could be very good at actually making the thing, and that's almost more important.

Stories about scientists

These spectacular stories will ignite your imagination and bring science vividly to life.

Mysterious laboratories, dangerous experiments, incredible inventions... whether it's classic science-fiction tales like *Frankenstein* or the action-packed adventures of Tony Stark and Bruce Banner, we love stories about scientists and their astonishing discoveries. Each of these five books takes a different approach, from exploring the fascinating lives of the real-life scientists whose work has shaped our history, to whisking us away on an adventure inspired by quantum physics. Even if science isn't your favourite subject, these books will blow your mind.

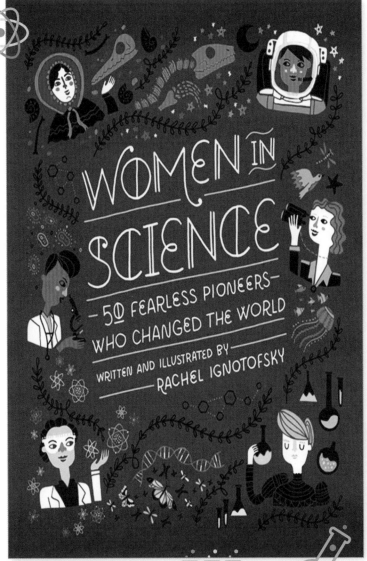

Women in Science
by Rachel Ignotofsky

(Hachette Children's Group)

This super-cool illustrated book brings together fun facts about 50 amazing female pioneers of science, technology, engineering and maths. Although there are some famous names among them, there are also plenty of inspiring innovators here who might be less familiar – from genius mathematicians such as Katherine Johnson (the woman behind the first manned Moon landing) to brilliant astronauts, fossil collectors, chemists and the ancient astronomer, Hypatia. Author Rachel Ignotofsky is also an illustrator and graphic designer, and has made every page of this book look fantastic.

The Many Worlds of Albie Bright
by Christopher Edge (Nosy Crow)

Soon after Albie's mum dies from cancer, he makes up his mind to undertake an unusual mission. Drawing on all he knows about quantum physics, and armed with his mum's old computer, a box and a banana, he sets out to visit parallel worlds – and maybe even find his mum again.

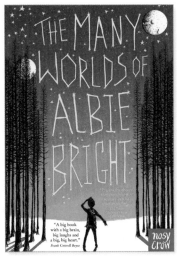

George's Secret Key to the Universe
by Lucy & Stephen Hawking

(Random House Children's Books)

Scientist Stephen Hawking has teamed up with his daughter Lucy to create this science-inspired series. When George meets his new neighbours, scientist Eric and his daughter Annie, he is plunged into an unexpected interplanetary adventure.

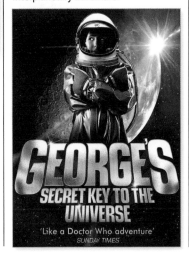

Little People, Big Dreams: Marie Curie
by Isabel Sanchez Vegara.
Illustrated by Frau Isa (Frances Lincoln)

This beautifully illustrated biography follows the inspiring real-life story of a famous scientist who discovered radium and polonium – two previously unknown elements (substances made from one type of atom) – and went on to win two Nobel Prizes.

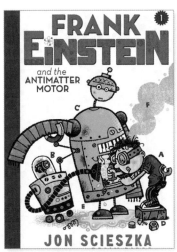

Frank Einstein and the Antimatter Motor
by Jon Scieszka.
Illustrated by Brian Biggs (Abrams)

Science whizz Frank is experimenting in his lab, when he unexpectedly brings two robots to life. Soon they are helping him build an anti-matter motor for his school science fair – but when Frank's arch-nemesis arrives on the scene, there's trouble in store for them all.

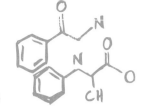

ANSWERS CAN BE FOUND ON PAGES 94–97

 # Science and technology

Wordsearch

Can you find all of these elements in the grid? Words may be hidden horizontally, vertically or diagonally, and reading either forwards or backwards.

ALUMINIUM
ARGON
BORON
BROMINE
CALCIUM
CARBON
CHLORINE
COBALT
COPPER
FLUORINE
GOLD
HELIUM
HYDROGEN
IODINE
IRON
KRYPTON
LEAD
LITHIUM
MAGNESIUM
MANGANESE

MERCURY
NEON
NICKEL
NITROGEN
OXYGEN
PHOSPHORUS
PLATINUM
PLUTONIUM
POTASSIUM
RADON
SILICON
SILVER
SODIUM
SULPHUR
TITANIUM
TUNGSTEN
URANIUM
XENON
ZINC
ZIRCONIUM

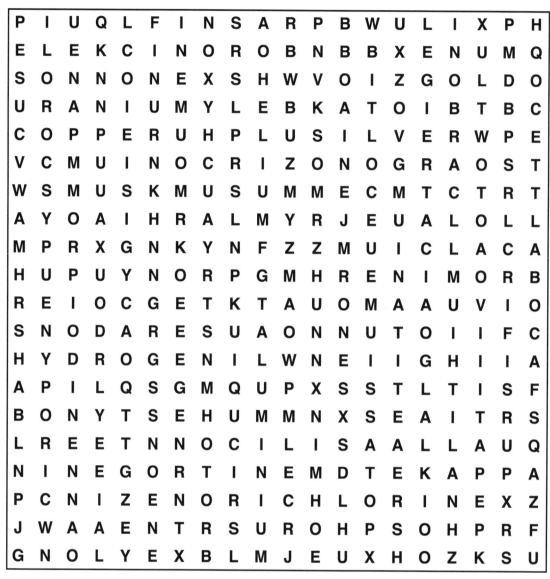

Sudoku

Place each number from 1–6 exactly once in each row, column and bold-lined 3x2 box. Can you complete the grid and solve the sudoku puzzle?

		1	4	6	
4	6		1		
	2	4			
			2	1	
	2			4	5
	4	5	3		

Code riddles

Each of these words relating to physics has had each letter replaced by the letter after it in the alphabet (so A becomes B, B becomes C and so on). Can you break the code to reveal the answers?

QBSUJDMF =

FMFDUSJDJUZ =

NBHOFU =

Number tower

Place a number in every square to complete the number tower. The value in each square is the sum of the numbers in the two squares directly beneath it.

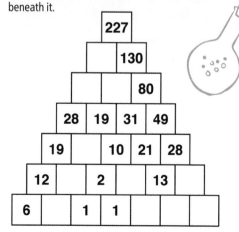

227
130
80
28 19 31 49
19 10 21 28
12 2 13
6 1 1

Number cross

All the numbers below appear exactly once in the puzzle grid. Can you work out where each one goes? We've placed one number to start you off.

4 numbers	8 numbers
1132	37284953
5192	62502384
5824	
6843	**11 numbers**
6999	16549748871
7923	99914697421

5 numbers	12 numbers
~~57417~~	111311449109
85429	386209230229
	701917956151
6 numbers	753267593149
149249	
838216	

7 numbers
5736625
9920864

Grid contains: 5 7 4 1 7

Anagrams

Rearrange the scrambled letters to form a body part.

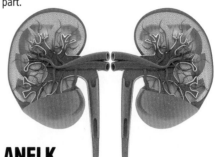

ANELK
(CLUE: Between your foot and your leg)

INKSDYE
(CLUE: Organs that filter waste products)

HAMCOST
(CLUE: Where you digest your food)

Keyword crossword

Once you have completed the crossword, use the letters in the highlighted boxes to form a word. Write it in the space below the clues.

Across
4. Famous landmark in Paris (6,5)
7. Uncontrollable fear or anxiety (5)
8. Break (4)
9. Change the order of items (9)
12. Military force (4)
14. Make happen (5)
15. Chance (11)

Down
1. Coat fastener (6)
2. Power that flows from a battery (11)
3. Chart (5)
5. Make-believe; not real life (7)
6. Come first (3)
8. Redness caused by being outside on a hot day (7)
10. Happenings (6)
11. Head of a town (5)
13. Diagram showing roads and places in an area (3)

Keyword clue: A science subject

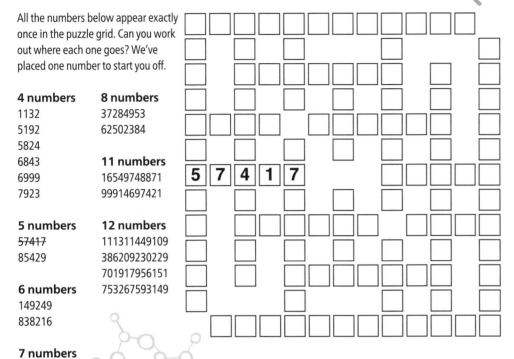

Spot the difference

Can you find the five differences between these pictures?

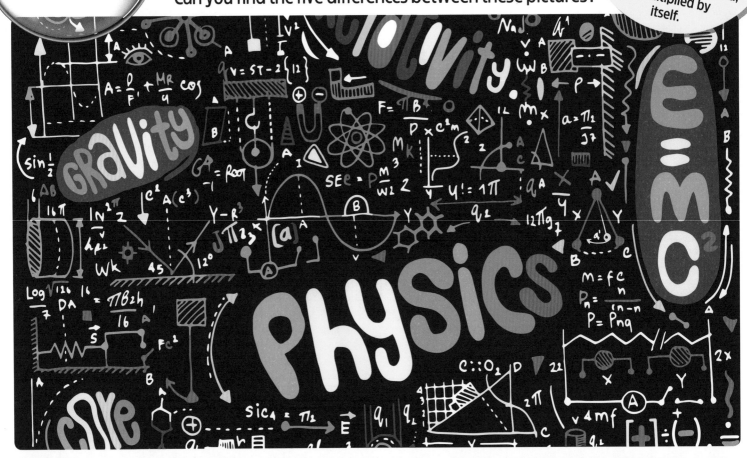

How to...
Be a scientist
Three ways to hone your scientific skills.

Science is not all high-tech laboratories and flashy multimillion-pound experiments – anyone who likes asking questions and working things out for themselves is already a scientist. Scientists figure out how the world works by looking closely, being curious and taking things apart. Stretch your science muscles with these three activities.

Look for clues

Biologists explore the environment to find out about living things. Test your observation skills by discovering what lives in your local park. Look under rocks and logs to find creatures that hide in the cool, damp darkness.

What you'll need
- Magnifying glass
- Notepad and pencil
- Nature-spotting guidebook
- Camera

What to look out for
- ☐ Fox droppings with a twisty point at one end.
- ☐ Holes in trees that have been made by woodpeckers.
- ☐ Nibbled nutshells or pine cones left near trees by squirrels.
- ☐ Hedgehog poo sparkling with broken beetle shell.

WARNING!
Make sure to take an adult with you on expeditions.

Do an experiment

Chemists look at substances and observe how they react with each other. Try this easy experiment and write down what happens.

What you'll need
- 2tsp baking powder
- 2tsp liquid hand soap
- Juice of 1 lemon
- Glass
- Spoon

What to do
1. Measure the baking powder into an empty glass.
2. Add the liquid soap and stir the mixture together.
3. Pour the lemon juice into the mixture.
4. Stir together and watch what happens.

Record your observations here:

What happens first of all?

Try adding another teaspoon of baking powder. What happens now?

How it works
When mixed, the baking soda and the citric acid in the lemon juice react to make carbon dioxide gas. This gas forms the bubbles.

Find patterns

Astronomers try to understand the wonders of the universe. Go out on a clear night and get far away from any bright lights. Can you spot the patterns of stars called constellations? Make stick models of these shapes using marshmallows and toothpicks.

What you'll need
- Bag of marshmallows
- Toothpicks

SAY WHAT?
"The important thing is not to stop questioning. Curiosity has its own reason for existing."
Albert Einstein

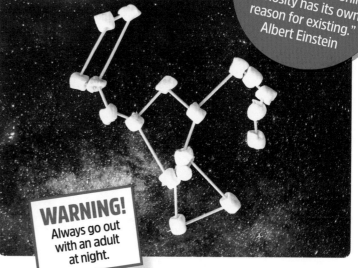

WARNING!
Always go out with an adult at night.

ARTS ENTERTA

From the secrets of the stage to the world's strangest art, discover

AND INMENT

the different ways humans tell stories and express themselves.

It's showtime!

Theatre is the art of performing stories.

If you've ever shouted "He's behind you!" at a pantomime at Christmas, laughed at the jokes in *Matilda the Musical*, or sung along to *Hakuna Matata* while watching *The Lion King* on stage, you'll know how exciting the theatre is. The reason that audiences find the theatre so engaging is partly because the performances are live, and therefore the experience of watching it is unique every time and can never be repeated exactly. Another important aspect of theatre is that it is collaborative, which means that people make it by working together.

Once upon a time...

Tribal dance and religious rituals from about 8500BC onwards contained some elements of theatre, but the theatre of today is shaped by traditions that began later, in ancient Greece. Most Greek cities had a theatre in the open air, usually on a hillside, with space for big audiences; some could hold more than 15,000 people. All the performers were men or boys. They performed as a group, called the chorus. Even in the late 16th century, during the time of William Shakespeare – probably the world's most famous playwright – female roles were still played by men or boys. It was not until 1660 that women started appearing on stage.

DID YOU KNOW?
A poet called Thespis in the 6th century BC became the first performer to speak as an individual, not a group, in the theatre. Actors call themselves "thespians" after him.

Matilda the Musical is based on a book by Roald Dahl.

That's entertainment

Plays in ancient Greece were either comedies or tragedies.

In ancient Greece, plays could be divided into comedies, which poke fun and make people laugh, or tragedies, which are serious and sad and make the audience think about right and wrong. These broad categories are still used today.

Performers in ancient Greece often wore masks and wigs. They also wore shoes with thick soles that made them look taller, and padded costumes that could make them look fatter or stronger. The masks would make it easier for the audience to work out which kind of character an actor was playing: funny, sad or angry. Sometimes, masks had two sides, which meant the actor could turn them round and change their mood for a scene.

It wasn't until the second half of the 19th century that actors started to portray situations that looked and sounded more like real life. These plays were called "cup and saucer dramas" but after the Second World War, they were replaced by "kitchen-sink drama", which usually showed the lives of ordinary people.

WOW!
The Mousetrap is the longest-running play in the theatre. It has now been performed continuously for over 60 years. It has a surprise ending so audiences are asked to keep it secret.

Musical theatre

Musicals are a very exciting and popular form of theatre. They are plays that contain singing and dancing as an essential part of the action, as well as spoken dialogue. Musicals combine many elements that are aimed at delighting audiences. These often include catchy songs that might be solo songs, duets (songs for two people) or choruses, for all the performers to sing together. In a musical, there will also usually be fabulous costumes, dance sequences and dazzling spectacles that will amaze the audience. *The Lion King*, *Matilda*, *Les Misérables* and *Cats* are all very popular musicals.

The Lion King.

THEATRE TALK
People who work in the theatre think it is bad luck to say "Good luck!" Instead they say "Break a leg!" No one knows exactly why.

Putting on a show

It is not just through language that drama is created in the theatre. It is a combination of costume, lighting, music, scenery sound, speeches and objects that actors hold, which are called props. Special effects are very sophisticated now, but in the time of Shakespeare, a storm effect could be conjured by beating a drum to make the sound of thunder, for example, and throwing powder into a candle flame to look like a lightning bolt.

Glossary

Cast People who perform in the show.

Crew All the people who work together on a show except the cast.

Lighting designer The person who designs the lighting for a show.

Scenery The backdrop used to represent the place where the action is unfolding.

Director The person who decides what the show will be like and works on this with cast and crew.

Ensemble A group of actors, singers or dancers who perform together on stage.

A bull with a big heart
Ferdinand (released December 2017) tells the tale of a bull who wants to find his family.

DID YOU KNOW?
This isn't Ferdinand's first screen appearance – he was the star of a short animation called *Ferdinand the Bull*, which was made by Walt Disney in 1938.

Behind the scenes
Wonder Woman star Gal Gadot on set with the film's director, Patty Jenkins.

Racing for victory
Cars 3 pits Lightning McQueen against an edgy young upstart called Jackson Storm.

Go Ninja!
The Lego Ninjago Movie stars six secret ninja warriors – and lots of brightly coloured bricks.

Comeback bear
In the follow-up to the first *Paddington* film, the bear from Peru sets out to catch a thief.

Pretty in pink
Katy Perry sings amid a sea of huge pompoms.

Stage and screen star
Ed Sheeran is seen from all angles on big screens on the Pyramid Stage at Glastonbury Festival in June 2017.

THAT'S STRANGE...
Ed Sheeran likes to give his guitars names. His collection includes Cyril, Felix, Trevor and James the Second.

The world's weirdest
ARTWORKS

Art can be funny, thought-provoking and sometimes downright strange.

When you think of art, you might think of old paintings or marble statues. Think again! It's not all dusty pictures of bowls of fruit or people from the past. Here are six of the world's oddest artworks.

Maman
by Louise Bourgeois

Louise Bourgeois spent her whole life as an artist, but it wasn't until she was in her 70s that the public really started to take notice of her work. Through her sculptures and paintings, she tried to understand humankind's basic needs: protection and being cared for. She was especially interested in spiders, which she thought of as friendly. *Maman*, which means mummy in French, is from a series of sculptures of the creepy crawlies that she created in the late 1990s. An enormous steel structure that stands more than nine metres high, *Maman* is a tribute to the artist's own mother. "Like spiders," she said, "My mother was very clever."

Bourgeois's steel spider towers over passers-by.

Lobster Telephone by Salvador Dalí

SWEET TALENT
Salvador Dalí might be most famous for his eccentric art, but his works weren't all weird – he also designed the logo for Chupa Chups lollies.

Salvador Dalí was a real eccentric. An exuberant Spaniard, he wore a long moustache, twirled up at the ends, and kept an anteater for a pet. He was a member of the Surrealist movement – a group of artists who thought they could unravel the secrets of the mind by painting dreams. By forming connections between totally unrelated things, they hoped to shock people into having new thoughts and ideas. One of Dalí's most famous sculptures is *Lobster Telephone*, made in 1936. It's an old-fashioned telephone, with a model lobster over the receiver. It was partly inspired by drawings he made following a trip to New York, US.

Paintings for the Temple
by Hilma af Klint

Abstract art is what we call artworks that aren't supposed to resemble anything in the world around us, but rather are intended to make us think or feel something. Many people believe that abstract art started with Wassily Kandinsky, but Hilma af Klint was painting her amazing abstracts years earlier – although that's not what's weird about her work. Af Klint was part of a group called The Five, who claimed to be in touch with spirits called The High Masters. The artist declared that it was one of these spirits who guided her hand and told her what to paint...

20:50 by Richard Wilson

The oil's shiny surface reflects the room.

Richard Wilson is an artist who specialises in making changes to rooms, or architecture, in order to make people feel uneasy. His work is often called installation, which means that rather than being a sculpture, for example, the artwork is designed especially to change the way in which a space – like a room or a courtyard – is experienced.

Wilson's most famous, and weirdest, work dates back to 1987. It's called *20:50*, and consists of a room completely flooded with shiny black oil. A walkway extends into the oily lagoon, and viewers can walk into it. The effect is disorientating; the perfectly still oil reflects the ceiling and walls of the room, so down becomes up, and up is down.

The Garden of Earthly Delights by Hieronymus Bosch

This section of the painting shows the Garden of Eden.

The oldest work on this list, Hieronymus Bosch's *The Garden of Earthly Delights* is one of the weirdest. Bosch was a painter who lived and worked in the Netherlands in the late 15th century. In those days, many people couldn't read, so art was a way of teaching people stories from the Bible through illustrations. That's exactly what *The Garden of Earthly Delights* sets out to do. It shows different Biblical scenes – from the Garden of Eden to the terrifying hell of the Last Judgement. What makes it so amazing are all the incredibly detailed, weird and wonderful creatures and people that are packed into the painting – all of them drawn from Bosch's bonkers imagination.

Fountain by Marcel Duchamp

Believe it or not, *Fountain,* by Marcel Duchamp, is one of the most important artworks of the 20th century. What is it? It's a urinal, signed R. Mutt and dated the year it was made: 1917. Duchamp's background was in painting, but he became more and more interested in finding out what art was, and what it could be. That's how he came to submit a urinal with the comical title *Fountain* to an exhibition. He was the first person to suggest that art didn't have to be a work of beauty or skill – that an object could be art if an artist says it is. This was a revolutionary idea – and one that continues to affect how artists work today.

A coach for animal actors

Julie Tottman trains pets to perform.

Julie Tottman has trained a lot of animals in her 22-year career. She's trained dogs to use the toilet, owls to deliver mail and squirrels to shell nuts. She has a wide variety of animal "actors" under her wing, and she's worked on films such as the *Harry Potter* movies, *Finding Neverland* and *The Dark Knight*.

It was Tottman's childhood dog, Sally, that ignited her passion for training animals. "I used to train my dog, much to everyone's disbelief, but it was just one of those things where it came naturally," she says.

She started her animal career working in a local pet beauty salon at 14 years old. In 1995, she got her big break when she was asked to work with animal trainer Gary Gero on the film *101 Dalmatians*.

In 1999, Gero and Tottman decided to set up the UK branch of Birds & Animals Unlimited – a company that provides animals and animal trainers to entertainment companies. The offers to

work on more films together started pouring in.

One of Tottman's biggest ever jobs was as head trainer on the *Harry Potter* films. "It was such a varied job," she says. "From the key animals such as Hagrid's dog, Fang, to Hermione's cat, Crookshanks, to the owls and even hippos for the moving portraits."

Out of all the animals that Tottman has had to train, though, she admits that training owls to deliver letters was one of the toughest. "What takes a raven a week to learn takes an owl two months," she says. "You start by showing them a letter and they'll ignore it. Then after a week they might nudge it with their beak."

Once the animals retire from work, Tottman says that the trainers often take them in. "I still have pets at home... they're all retired animal actors. I'm convinced we have enough room for them all. My partner might not say the same thing, though," she says.

STAR TURNS
In her 11 years working on *Harry Potter*, Tottman says she helped train around 250 animals.

Animal trainers must be patient.

Tottman trained animals for the *Harry Potter* films.

SCARY SPIDERS
Tottman doesn't like spiders so, when filming *Harry Potter and the Chamber of Secrets*, she couldn't go on the set the day that 200 tarantulas were delivered.

WOW!
"I've written a couple of books that can talk you through all the tricks. They are called *Superstar Dogs* and *Superstar Cats*," says Tottman.

Q&A

Julie Tottman

The Week Junior talks to Tottman about what it is like to train her animals.

What is your favourite film you have worked on?
That was probably *102 Dalmatians*. I was the head puppy trainer so was paid to play with puppies every day for four months. They loved learning new tricks and all the attention they got on set. The most puppies we ever had at one time was 30. We would film them multiple times to make it look like there were lots and lots.

Have any of the animals been naughty on set?
As you can imagine, puppies

can be very cheeky, and once in a while would run off and play instead. This, of course, was ok as they were babies, and if they wanted play or nap time, they got it.

If you could be an animal what animal would you be?
I think I would be a dog. My dogs get so much love and lots of tasty treats.

What does training an animal involve?
Lots of patience. You must never get cross. It is all about love and confidence and ensuring the animal enjoys it.

Keeping things simple and being consistent is the key. I use hand signals, as when we are filming, I am not allowed to talk.

What is the hardest trick you've had to teach an animal?
That would be getting a cat to retrieve an object. It takes weeks and weeks. I had to do it for *Harry Potter*.

How does someone become an animal trainer?
It's hard to get into, but I'd advise doing an animal-behaviour course and work experience with a film trainer.

WARNER BROS - PA PHOTOS

Books behind blockbusters

Lots of big films started life as page-turners. Which have you read?

You've seen it at the cinema – but have you read the book? Whether it's *Harry Potter*, *The Hunger Games*, *Mary Poppins* or *The Wizard of Oz*, lots of popular films take their original inspiration from children's books. Although the movies may bring the magic of these stories to life on the big screen, there's nothing quite like curling up with the original story and letting your imagination get to work. So find somewhere comfortable to settle down and enjoy delving into these five books that have inspired blockbuster movies – then decide which is better, the book or the film.

Michael Bond

A Bear Called Paddington

DID YOU KNOW?
More than 35 million Paddington books have been sold worldwide.

Illustrated by Peggy Fortnum

The first adventures of Paddington Bear

A Bear Called Paddington
by Michael Bond

(HarperCollins Children's Books)

When Mr and Mrs Brown go to collect their daughter from Paddington Station, they are surprised to find instead a bear from darkest Peru, bearing a label that reads "PLEASE LOOK AFTER THIS BEAR". From then on their lives will never be quite the same. If you enjoyed the film, you'll love the original story about the bear that the actor and comedian Stephen Fry has described as "a great British institution".

The Hundred and One Dalmatians
by Dodie Smith.
Illustrated by David Robert

(Egmont)

When their puppies are kidnapped by the evil Cruella de Vil, it's down to Pongo and Missis to rescue them. This classic story has appeared on TV and in cinemas, but the original book is a real treat – charming, funny and exciting.

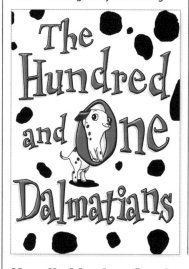

Howl's Moving Castle
by Diana Wynne Jones

(HarperCollins Children's Books)

You might have seen the award-winning Studio Ghibli animated film, but did you know it was based on a children's book by Diana Wynne Jones? When Sophie is put under a spell by the terrible Witch of the Waste, she seeks refuge in the mysterious moving castle in the hills, home of the feared Wizard Howl.

How to Train Your Dragon
by Cressida Cowell

(Hachette Children's Books)

Hiccup Horrendous Haddock the Third isn't your typical Viking hero, but in this, the first book about his adventures, he manages to capture a toothless dragon and tries to train it. Fans of the animation may be surprised to see how much the book differs from the film.

A Wrinkle in Time
by Madeleine L'Engle

(Puffin Books)

It's not yet hit cinema screens, but the brand new adaptation of a classic science-fiction adventure is set to be one of the most anticipated movies of 2018. Get ahead by discovering the captivating story of Meg and her little brother Charles, who go searching for their lost father.

Wordsearch

Can you find all the book, film and show names that are hidden in the grid? Words may be hidden horizontally, vertically or diagonally, and reading either forwards or backwards.

ANSWERS CAN BE FOUND ON PAGES 94–97

P	T	M	Y	T	H	E	C	A	T	I	N	T	H	E	H	A	T	O	H
M	A	T	I	L	D	A	E	T	H	E	L	I	O	N	K	I	N	G	Z
A	T	H	E	B	F	G	I	S	E	H	C	T	I	W	E	H	T	S	C
A	B	E	W	S	E	T	T	O	L	R	A	H	C	R	A	H	I	F	U
Y	O	B	E	R	I	A	N	O	I	L	L	I	B	M	E	T	A	Q	T
N	M	O	L	M	T	Y	U	N	T	P	R	O	A	J	H	N	D	H	R
N	E	R	T	A	H	R	A	B	T	E	L	M	U	E	T	A	E	A	A
A	N	R	T	R	E	O	L	A	L	B	M	N	P	A	D	L	S	R	C
R	G	O	I	Y	T	T	U	M	E	A	G	O	S	E	E	L	P	R	Y
G	N	W	L	P	W	S	F	B	M	L	L	T	D	G	M	E	I	Y	B
A	I	E	T	O	I	Y	W	I	E	A	I	T	O	A	O	R	C	P	E
T	D	R	R	P	T	O	A	B	R	C	O	M	L	U	N	E	A	O	A
S	N	S	A	P	S	T	O	E	M	S	O	M	B	Y	D	D	B	T	K
G	I	I	U	I	V	O	X	R	A	V	F	R	O	Z	E	N	L	T	E
N	F	N	T	N	K	P	F	N	I	D	D	A	L	A	N	I	E	E	R
A	P	G	S	S	R	O	M	E	D	S	L	L	O	R	T	C	M	R	H
G	P	G	E	E	X	T	O	I	L	L	E	Y	L	L	I	B	E	E	S
R	U	A	S	O	N	I	D	D	O	O	G	E	H	T	S	R	A	C	B
D	E	S	I	O	T	R	O	T	C	N	I	S	R	E	T	S	N	O	M
F	T	H	E	G	R	U	F	F	A	L	O	N	A	P	R	E	T	E	P

ALADDIN	MONSTERS INC
AWFUL AUNTIE	PETER PAN
BAMBI	SHREK
BILLIONAIRE BOY	SING
BILLY ELLIOT	STUART LITTLE
BLOB	THE BFG
CARS	THE BORROWERS
CHARLOTTE'S WEB	THE CAT IN THE HAT
CINDERELLA	THE GOOD DINOSAUR
DEMON DENTIST	THE GRUFFALO
DESPICABLE ME	THE JUNGLE BOOK
ESIO TROT	THE LEGO MOVIE
FANTASTIC MR FOX	THE LION KING
FINDING NEMO	THE LITTLE MERMAID
FROZEN	THE POLAR EXPRESS
GANGSTA GRANNY	THE TWITS
HARRY POTTER	THE WITCHES
MAMMA MIA	TOY STORY
MARY POPPINS	TRACY BEAKER
MATILDA	TROLLS

Sudoku

Place the numbers from 1–6 exactly once in each row, column and 3x2 bold-lined box. Can you complete the grid and solve the sudoku puzzle?

	5	3		1	2
1					5
	4				
					4
4					1
	2	5	4	6	

Code riddles

Each of these author names has had each letter replaced by the letter after it in the alphabet (so B becomes A, C becomes B and so on).

SPBME EBIM =

CFBUSJY QPUUFS =

MFXJT DBSSPMM =

Number tower

Place a number in every square to complete the number tower. The value in each square is the sum of the numbers in the two squares directly beneath it.

		231			
	55		55		
	30		25		
18		13			
			8	9	10
5	6	1	4	4	5

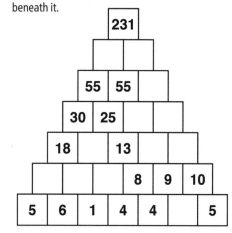

UNIVERSAL STUDIOS

Number cross

All the numbers below appear exactly once in the puzzle grid. Can you work out where each one goes? We've placed one number to start you off.

3 numbers	6 numbers
471	146319
543	157444
641	454667
872	478725
	507683
4 numbers	754417
1291	779755
2426	947574
4093	
4575	**7 numbers**
5746	1365064
6570	4879408
	5173974
	5240357
	~~7498917~~
	7655484

8 numbers	9 numbers
55636670	148708579
70693375	905603599

Grid pre-placed digits (top right column): 7, 4, 9, 8, 9, 1, 7

Anagrams

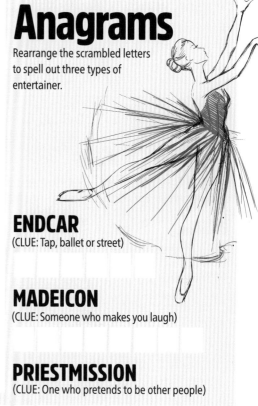

Rearrange the scrambled letters to spell out three types of entertainer.

ENDCAR
(CLUE: Tap, ballet or street)

MADEICON
(CLUE: Someone who makes you laugh)

PRIESTMISSION
(CLUE: One who pretends to be other people)

Keyword crossword

Once you have completed the crossword, use the letters in the highlighted boxes to form a word. Write it in the space below the clues.

Across
1. Thick and strong paper (9)
6. Lift up (5)
7. Collection of songs released by a band (5)
9. Coins of low value (7)
12. Opposite of deep (7)
16. Lemonade or water, for instance (5)
17. Outside part of an egg (5)
18. Admired or highly regarded (9)

Down
2. Precipitation (4)
3. Short high-pitched sound (5)
4. Once more or a second time (5)
5. Capital of Ireland (6)
6. Prepared for exams (7)
8. ___ instrument: for example a trombone or recorder (7)
10. A strong sense of self-worth (3)
11. Less difficult (6)
13. Small bodies of water (5)
14. Rubbish (5)
15. Regular rhythm in music (4)

Keyword clue: Surname of an author

Spot the difference

Can you find the five differences between the pictures?

HOW TO...
Make your own music

You don't need instruments or high-tech gear to create your own terrific tunes.

Follow our tips for songwriting success and discover some apps to help you compose music. It doesn't matter which order you do it in – some people start with the song and others begin by coming up with a catchy tune.

Songwriting tips

Write from experience
Some of the best songs are by singers who wrote about their personal experience. Taylor Swift says, "My experience with songwriting is usually so confessional." If you put your feelings into writing a song then other people will feel it, too.

Don't worry if it takes a long time
Trying to find a good hook for your song may take a while. Famous songwriter, Rod Stewart, said that sometimes he would only write one line of lyrics a day.

Get all the bad stuff out first
Don't worry if the first few songs you write are rubbish. Ed Sheeran said that he wrote lots of terrible songs before he got to the good stuff.

Ask for feedback
Perform your song for someone and see what they think. Ask for ways you can improve it, and it will only get better.

Try writing your own song here:

SONGWRITER TO THE STARS
Ed Sheeran writes all his own songs – but he's also written songs for Justin Bieber, Olly Murs, One Direction, Taylor Swift and The Weeknd.

Music-making apps

HumOn Android (Free)
As you may have guessed from its name, HumOn relies on the easiest form of music-making: humming. It allows anyone to make music without the need for instruments. To use it, all you have to do is hum a tune into your phone's microphone. HumOn listens to your notes and turns it into a proper musical score on screen. You can also tell the app to play your tune in different styles, such as ballad, classical, R&B and rock.

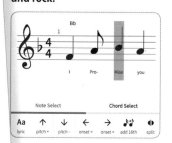

Groovebox iOS (Free)
Groovebox is an app that allows you to make dance music on an iPhone or iPad. The app is divided into three sections: Drumbox for beats, Retrobass for basslines and Poly-8 for the melody that sits on top. Your job is to use them (in any order you like) to make a tune. Drums are easy; you hit a record button and then tap the different sounds with your fingers to create a pattern.

GarageBand iOS (Free)
If you feel confident enough in your music to head straight to the recording studio, then Apple's GarageBand might be just the app for you. It features a collection of instrument sounds, such as guitars and keyboards, that you can use to make your own backing tracks. Once you've created a beat you like, you can add words on top.

BALL GAME

Visitors were trying new Nintendo Switch games at the Electronic and Entertainment Expo (E3) in Los Angeles, US, on 13 June 2017. At the Nyko exhibition, gamers got to play Mario Kart while lying in a ball pit. Mario Kart 8 Deluxe, which came out in 2017, has sold more than 3.5 million copies on the Switch and is the fastest-selling game in the popular racing series.

ON SCREEN

If you're a big fan of games, turn the page to find out about some of the most successful titles in history.

Digital playground

Video games have been around since 1958, so what's next in the digital world?

In 1983, a Japanese playing-card company named Nintendo brought out a device that would become the first mainstream home console to become popular all over the world. From that first Nintendo Entertainment System (NES), right up to the latest consoles, video gaming has evolved with changing technology.

Today, you can play games anywhere, in any way, and on almost anything. It's not just that the devices on which people play are more powerful, the way in which they are playing is changing, too. Whether it involves putting on a virtual-reality headset to ride a rollercoaster, or tracking down Pokémon in a real-life local park, players are being immersed in games in ways that didn't exist until very recently.

GO PLAY
Pokémon Go hit a peak of 45 million daily active users in July 2016.

Augmented reality

Augmented reality (AR) blurs the line between reality and fantasy by laying computer graphics onto real-world situations. AR has boomed as smartphones have become more powerful, allowing these graphics to be conjured in an instant. The biggest success of AR to date has been Pokémon Go. This game, which was released in 2016, makes it possible to catch Pokémon in real-world settings using GPS and your phone's camera. It has been downloaded 750 million times worldwide.

Milestones of gaming

1983: NINTENDO ENTERTAINMENT SYSTEM (NES)

The Famicom (short for family computer) console was first released in Japan in 1983. It was redesigned as Nintendo Entertainment System (NES) in 1985, introducing the world to a plumber named Mario. NES was the highest-selling console in North America at the time.

1989: NINTENDO GAME BOY

The ancestor of the 3DS and 2DS, this 1989 handheld device allowed people to take games on the move. Its rivals only lasted a few hours on a full set of batteries but the Game Boy could go on for up to 15 hours. It was released in the UK in 1990 and came with a bundled copy of Tetris. Its original price in the US was the equivalent of £144 now.

WOW!
Rez Infinite VR is based on a game released in 2001 for the PS2 and Sega Dreamcast consoles.

Virtual reality

Although Nintendo released the unsuccessful Virtual Boy headset in 1995, it is only recently that virtual reality (VR) – the idea of submerging yourself in a virtual world – has properly entered our homes. The Oculus Rift headset restarted the trend in 2010, and now there has been an explosion of VR, with hundreds of companies developing experiences. The technology hasn't been smooth sailing. Users often complain VR can make them feel sick if they play for too long, and despite Google releasing a cheap cardboard headset for phones, many VR experiences are still seen as too expensive.

What's next?

Everyone wants to feel like they're inside a game. So the next development is a full-body suit – if someone pokes you in a game, you really feel it. Developers are also working on discarding VR headsets. Microsoft's Illumiroom projects images and extensions of your gaming to your surrounding room. It can create holographic snow or rain projections on your floor.

Illumiroom changes how your home looks.

EVIL MARIO
Nintendo's heroic plumber Mario started out as a villain who had imprisoned a character called Donkey Kong. He was originally known as Jumpman.

1994-2017: SONY PLAYSTATION VS MICROSOFT XBOX

Sony and Microsoft became gaming giants by making each console more advanced than the last. The first PlayStation came out in the UK in 1995; it was the first console designed to focus on the 3D graphics we know today. The first Xbox arrived in 2002 and was a pioneer in online console gaming.

2006: NINTENDO WII

Although the Wii couldn't beat its rivals on graphics, Nintendo created a massive gaming trend in 2006 with motion control, selling more than 101 million consoles worldwide. People gradually got bored of playing like this, but many games nowadays, such as Splatoon 2, still have motion-control elements. Find out more about how the Wii works on page 71.

2017: NINTENDO SWITCH

The newest console revolutionised the gaming market in 2017. You can now go from taking your game out on a tablet to playing that same game on your TV just seconds later. It's not as powerful as its PlayStation 4 and Xbox One rivals, but it's much more versatile.

NINTENDO · THE POKEMON COMPANY · SONY ENTERTAINMENT

Playing together
Game lovers gather in the family and friends area at Gamescom 2017.

GAMERS' PARADISE
The photos on these pages were taken at Gamescom – Europe's largest computer games fair. It is held in Cologne, Germany, and was launched in 2009.

In the driving seat
A gamer is immersed in a race using a VR headset.

The green room
Xbox shows off its new games and consoles.

Dress to impress
People come in costume as their favourite game characters.

Rebel alliance
Star Wars fans play Star Wars Battlefront II at the EA stand.

Case off
Gamers at the event customise their computers. This one looks like a Dalek from *Doctor Who*.

Spectacular stands
Many of the stands showed amazing models, such as this fearsome dragon.

6 top-selling video games

Here are some of the most popular video games ever made. How many have you played?

WOW! It's thought that nearly 500 million copies of Tetris have been sold.

Tetris

This classic puzzle game is as simple as it gets. Shapes made of four square blocks known as "tetrominoes" fall from the top of the screen, and it's your job to arrange them so that they form horizontal lines. The game ends when the blocks reach the top of the screen. The simplicity of the game means that anyone can get the hang of it in just a few minutes. It also leaves you tantalisingly convinced that if you have just one more go, you can beat your top score. We almost didn't get the chance to play it, though. It was created in 1984 by a developer called Alexey Pajitnov, in Moscow, Russia (then part of the Soviet Union). Unfortunately, there was a difficulty: it was almost impossible for people to start their own business in the Soviet Union, so he had to give control of the game to the government. Eventually, in 1987, the Soviet leaders allowed publishers around the world to release it for all sorts of consoles and computers.

Super Mario Bros

CLASSIC CHARACTER Classic 2D Mario games are still going strong, as shown by the New Super Mario Bros series.

The Nintendo Entertainment System (called the Family Computer or Famicom in its home country of Japan) was a huge hit, selling around 60 million consoles around the globe. Much of this success is down to a pair of jumping plumbers – more than 40 million people owned the Super Mario Bros cartridge. When it came out in 1985, many people considered video games to be a dying fad because there were so many bad ones around, but once people had experienced Mario, public opinion changed. The game was huge for its time, with lots of enemies and almost as many ways of defeating them, and Mario became one of the most recognisable characters in the world. Mario Odyssey recently arrived on the Switch.

Pokémon Red and Blue

Gamers the world over went crazy over Pokémon Go in 2016 but when the first Pokémon Go games came out, not many people even realised. That's because despite being released for the Game Boy in February 1996 in Japan, the games weren't translated into English until 1998, and weren't sold in the UK until 1999. However, once global gamers had the chance to play it, they all thought, "Gotta catch 'em all!" as they explored, battled and found the monsters. The game looked basic, but many consider this part of the appeal, by stimulating players' own creativity and imagination. More than 31 million copies of these first Pokémon games were sold.

SWAP!
The first Pokémon games were released before the advent of online gaming, but Game Boy Pokémon players were able to connect their handheld consoles with a cable to battle and swap Pokémon.

The Sims

DID YOU KNOW?
The Sims was originally going to be based on designing homes and buying furniture, with people judging your choices, but the team realised that controlling the characters was the most fun part.

Children in the 1980s had a game called Little Computer People, which was about helping one man in a one-screen, three-storey house. It inspired a game designer called Will Wright who, in 2000, released The Sims. In the game, you must spend money to create a home and look after the family in it. You must ensure they go to work, get the right amount of sleep, wash themselves, eat food and even go to the toilet. If you cause a child in the game to get poor grades, they are sent away to a military school. Gamers found all these chores a lot of fun – the original sold 16 million copies, and went on to sell more than 52 million worldwide.

Minecraft

Inspired by a childhood playing Lego, Markus Persson wanted to create a video game that was just as open-ended. When Minecraft was released in 2009, it was an unexpected hit and its popularity just kept growing. Unlike most hit games, Minecraft was originally made by just one person, rather than a large team of developers and artists. So far, 107 million copies have been sold around the world – second only to Tetris. Although a major part of the game is to battle monsters and stay alive, the reason it became such a hit is because players love to build all sorts of things and make their own fun, just like you can with Lego.

Wii Sports

Until 2006, sports video games just had you sitting down and pushing buttons. However, Wii Sports and its console changed the way we looked at games. Covering baseball, bowling, boxing, golf and tennis, the game required players to hold a controller and actually perform the moves they would in real life. So to hit the ball back, you needed to swing your arm as if you were holding a tennis racquet. Thanks to the games' simplicity, many millions of people who weren't normally gamers played Wii Sports. It sold nearly 83 million copies – partly because a copy came with almost every Wii console sold.

A knack for game ideas

How game creator Mark Cerny became a hit.

A video game can be made anywhere in the world, but Japan still remains the most important place anywhere for consoles. With the exception of the Xbox range, every globally popular console of the past 30 years was designed and created in Japan – and it's hard for any outsider to be successful in its console industry. It takes a special talent.

Mark Cerny fits that bill. He's the main man behind the huge new PlayStation 4 release, Knack II. It's a console he knows plenty about. Sony wanted to create a console that developers could get the best out of, so the company decided it needed a developer to oversee the creation of the PS4 – and who better than Cerny?

Cerny was already a big deal. He finished school at 15 and went to study physics at university but dropped out. Just a few months after his 17th birthday, he was working for Atari, then considered the world's best arcade-game manufacturer. "I suppose my parents were a bit distressed with my career choice because they're both PhD students and they worked as scientists," Cerny says. "I think they were worried about all of the things that parents are normally worried about, like whether I would be able to make a living."

His first big game for Atari was called Marble Madness, and the arcade cabinet had a ball as a controller. He was just 18 at this time, and his game was the year's top seller. At 21, he moved to Japan to work for Sega, and later found himself producing Sonic The Hedgehog 2, perhaps the best Sonic game ever.

After leaving Sega, Cerny ended up focusing on games for the PlayStation consoles. He created games and characters people still remember and enjoy today, such as Ratchet & Clank and Crash Bandicoot. It's that legacy and know-how that led to the Knack series.

The surprise is that Cerny, now 53, wasn't inspired by games like this when he was young. "You couldn't play games like kids can nowadays," he says. "If you were interested in games, you'd have to go to the science museum and use their technology. It didn't occur to anyone that this would be a job." So next time you find yourself playing Knack II, just think, Cerny pretty much created the PS4 so he could make games like this.

ILLUSTRATIONS: 2015 USBORNE PUBLISHING LTD. PHOTOS: WIRED/CONDE NAST - REX SHUTTERSTOCK

EXPERT ADVICE
"Making games is not something you need to go to school to find out how to do... if you want to do it, you can do it," says Cerny.

Cerny has been making games since he was 17.

Q&A

Mark Cerny

The Knack II creator on playing and making games.

How much time did you spend playing games when making Knack II?
I'm either not playing games at all or I'll be playing for 12 hours straight. For example, I'll have to have the volume up really high to test the audio. Playing games in this way can make you feel really shattered.

How did your team work together on this game?
My job as a director revolves around making character action games. We normally have conferences, one after the other, because there are a million decisions to make with a game like Knack II, from colours, attacks, polygons and animations. The job of the creative director is to work out what the game will look like and decide the feel of the location. Then, there's the storyboard artists and the writers, too.

What snacks do you eat when you're at work?
In Tokyo, I tend to be really busy. I don't snack at all. In the morning I have two cups of tea and some granola. I don't have a favourite lunch and I don't like eating out when I'm in my hometown because I'm on the road for 165 days a year.

Do you always work in Japan or can you do your job elsewhere?
If I'm working from home, I'll be in LA, in the US, where I live. At home I have to use a special piece of equipment called a PS4 devkit (development kit). You can't buy one as they haven't been released in the shops. I also need a 40GB internet connection, which is a lot!

Guides to gaming and coding

These books could help you become the next big thing in programming.

If you're a fan of gaming, you'll be used to looking online for all the news about the latest games, the best tips and tricks, and maybe even gaming with your friends. Don't forget about books, though; they can offer a great way to discover the stats and information behind the technology, or to explore the beautiful artwork from your favourite games. What's more, if you're ever fancied learning more about coding, you'll find plenty of great books to guide you through the process of building your own websites, games and more. These five books are the perfect place to start.

Lift-the-Flap: Computers and Coding
by Rosie Dickins. Illustrated by Shaw Nielsen

(Usborne Publishing)

Find out all you need to know about computers and coding with this book, which explains even difficult concepts in a fun and straightforward way. The colourful pages are full of cute characters, cartoon-style illustrations, flaps to lift and quirky facts to discover. Puzzles and games help provide an insight into what goes on inside a computer and how computer languages work. You'll also find lots of links to more content online, including coding activities, games and tips.

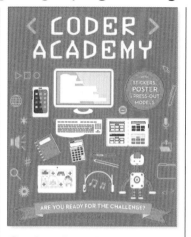

Coder Academy
by Sean McManus.
Illustrated by Rosan Magar

(Ivy Kids)

This new book, written by tech expert Sean McManus, will take you through a series of activities set up to help you learn both HTML and Scratch. Design your own character and animate it; make a digital instrument; build your own website and create a game. This book also comes with fun extras, such as stickers, a poster and 3D robots.

Coding for Beginners Using Scratch
by Rosie Dickins, Jonathan Melmoth and Louie Stowell. Illustrated by Shaw Nielsen

(Usborne Publishing)

Master Scratch with this beginner-friendly book. Starting with the basics, it will take you step by step through a series of fun projects, such as creating a virtual pet. This great guide will help you take your first steps in coding.

Minecraft: Blockopedia

(Egmont Publishing)

There are plenty of Minecraft books out there, but this fabulous encyclopaedia is something very special. Shaped like a 3D hexagonal Minecraft block, it's jam-packed with information about each and every type of block, including statistics, need-to-know facts and fun trivia. Written with input from expert gamer Alex Wiltshire, it's a detailed and thorough companion to the game – essential reading for any enthusiast.

Pokémon Deluxe Essential Handbook
by Cris Silvestri

(Scholastic)

If you love Pokémon, then you shouldn't be without this handbook, which contains pictures, essential stats and fun facts on more than 700 Pokémon. It's more of a collector's handbook than a strategy guide, but this is a great reference for Pokémon trainers to have on hand while playing.

Wordsearch

 ANSWERS CAN BE FOUND ON PAGES 94–97

Can you find all of these tech words and phrases in the grid? Words may be hidden horizontally, vertically or diagonally, and reading either forwards or backwards.

AMAZON FIRE
ANGRY BIRDS
CANDY CRUSH SAGA
CHAT ROOM
COMMENT
COMPUTER
CUT THE ROPE
CYBERSPACE
DRAW SOMETHING
EBOOK
EMAIL
FOLLOWERS
FRUIT NINJA
GOOGLE
HASHTAG
HEADPHONES
INTERNET
IPAD
JOYSTICK
JUST DANCE

KEYBOARD
KINDLE
LAPTOP
MINECRAFT
MONITOR
MOUSE
PLAYSTATION
POKEMON GO
PRINTER
SEARCH ENGINE
SMARTWATCH
SPEAKERS
STAR WARS
SURFING
TABLET
TEMPLE RUN
TOUCHSCREEN
TRENDING
WEBSITE
XBOX

T	I	R	S	B	I	K	N	U	R	E	L	P	M	E	T	U	Y	I	W
T	V	R	X	M	Y	Y	M	I	J	M	O	O	R	T	A	H	C	S	U
S	T	A	R	W	A	R	S	P	A	K	V	J	W	B	Y	R	U	P	T
Z	F	A	P	D	U	R	W	R	E	T	U	P	M	O	C	E	A	F	O
X	W	R	G	R	W	C	T	M	V	S	P	O	E	R	E	S	K	T	H
S	R	E	S	A	I	O	O	W	T	L	U	F	R	H	T	U	V	A	T
E	Q	Q	B	W	S	N	Q	D	A	S	T	G	S	E	A	R	R	V	P
N	P	R	Y	S	G	H	A	Y	E	T	I	A	D	N	B	F	K	R	Y
O	T	O	E	O	I	N	S	C	O	F	C	T	R	I	L	I	I	A	I
H	E	U	R	M	C	T	D	U	T	A	F	H	I	G	E	N	P	M	Y
P	N	D	K	E	A	R	E	E	R	R	D	S	B	N	T	G	D	A	X
D	R	R	C	T	H	I	S	L	U	C	R	A	Y	E	N	O	F	Z	D
A	E	A	I	H	Z	T	L	I	D	E	Y	H	R	H	E	O	O	O	S
E	T	O	T	I	X	I	T	R	T	N	N	D	G	C	M	G	L	N	R
H	N	B	S	N	X	N	C	U	W	I	I	E	N	R	M	L	L	F	O
P	I	Y	Y	G	I	O	S	E	C	M	Y	K	A	A	O	E	O	I	T
F	M	E	O	N	C	Y	B	E	R	S	P	A	C	E	C	S	W	R	I
N	A	K	J	S	U	O	P	X	T	O	U	C	H	S	C	R	E	E	N
X	L	A	P	T	O	P	T	A	M	R	G	N	I	D	N	E	R	T	O
I	J	U	W	K	W	Q	A	Y	O	S	R	E	K	A	E	P	S	A	M

Sudoku

Place the numbers from 1–6 exactly once in each row, column and 3x2 bold-lined box. Can you complete the grid and solve the sudoku puzzle?

	2	5			
			6	2	
3	5		2		
		6		5	3
	4	3			
				3	4

Code riddles

Each of these words relating to social media has had each letter replaced by the letter after it in the alphabet (so A becomes B, B becomes C and so on). Can you break the code to reveal the answers?

JOTUBHSBN =

UXJUUFS =

GBDFCPPL =

Number tower

Place a number in every square to complete the number tower. The value in each square is the sum of the numbers in the two squares directly beneath it.

		235		
		104		
	69	62	42	
	35	34		
		18	10	
13		10		2
10	3	3		1	1

Number cross

All the numbers below appear exactly once in the puzzle grid. Can you work out where each one goes? We've placed one number to start you off.

4 numbers
1725
4718
5719
7831

7 numbers
1121627
2604784
4461839
6413021

5 numbers
14616
27737
79151
82651

8 numbers
13708560
20433455
42469584
79750635

6 numbers
106170
823206
851853
979828

12 numbers
181955619118
567858092606
821112522263
916293235801

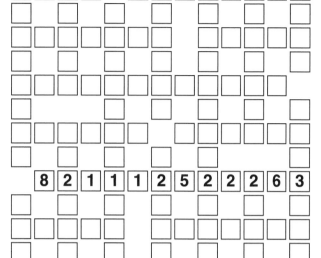

Anagrams

Rearrange the scrambled letters to form words relating to computers.

ALIME
(CLUE: Quicker than sending letters)

SWAPSROD
(CLUE: Use this to stay secure)

TWOFEARS
(CLUE: This runs on computers)

Keyword crossword

Once you have completed the crossword, use the letters in the highlighted boxes to form a word. Write it in the space below the clues.

Across
1. In the end (10)
6. Not new (4)
7. Cause to feel very enthusiastic (6)
8. Not present (6)
9. Soft metal (4)
11. Camera part (4)
13. Anticipate something will happen (6)
15. Very thin rope (6)
17. Require (4)
18. Space travellers (10)

Down
2. Able to be seen (7)
3. Prod gently (5)
4. Nearby (5)
5. Until now (3)
7. Consume food (3)
10. Very old (7)
12. Rapid or fast (5)
13. A chicken might lay one (3)
14. Black and white mammal (5)
16. Popular drink (3)

Keyword clue: Electronic device

Spot the difference

Can you find the five differences between these pictures?

HOW TO...

Customise your phone case

Phone cases are practical but that doesn't mean they have to be dull.

What you'll need

- Newspaper
- Nail varnish (various colours)
- Straws
- Plain phone case

Start by covering your work surface with something that will protect it, such as newspaper – things are about to get messy. Put the case in the centre of the newspaper. Line up the different coloured nail varnishes and pop a straw next to each of them. Dip a straw into the first nail varnish.

Hover the straw over the case and blow gently through the other end. Do this a few times until there are lots of splatters on your case. Do the same with the other straws and colours until your case is covered in colourful splatters. Leave to dry completely and then pop the case on your phone.

DRIP PAINTING
American artist Jackson Pollock was known for his unusual style of painting. Pollock dripped paint onto canvas to create swirly lines and splatters.

WOW!
The first call on a mobile phone was made in New York, US, in 1973.

Three more creative cases

Colourful critters
Customise a transparent or white phone case by drawing insects crawling across it. For the best results, use fine-tip permanent markers. Ladybirds and bees will look particularly nice and bright.

Mapped out
Personalise your case by decorating it with a map of a place that means something to you. Either print it off or ask permission to cut up an old map. Trim to fit then pop it inside the case with the map facing out. Your phone will hold it in place.

Terrific tattoos
Did you know that temporary tattoos work on phone cases, too? Pick a design you like and transfer it onto the case. Then paint over the tattoo with clear nail varnish to make it last longer.

PAINT THE TOWN...

Children in Sussex, England, take part in the Colour the Coast fun run along the seafront. Runners passed through four colour zones, where helpers known as cherry chuckers showered entrants with dye before a finish-line party, where everyone threw coloured powder into the sky to create a rainbow-hued cloud.

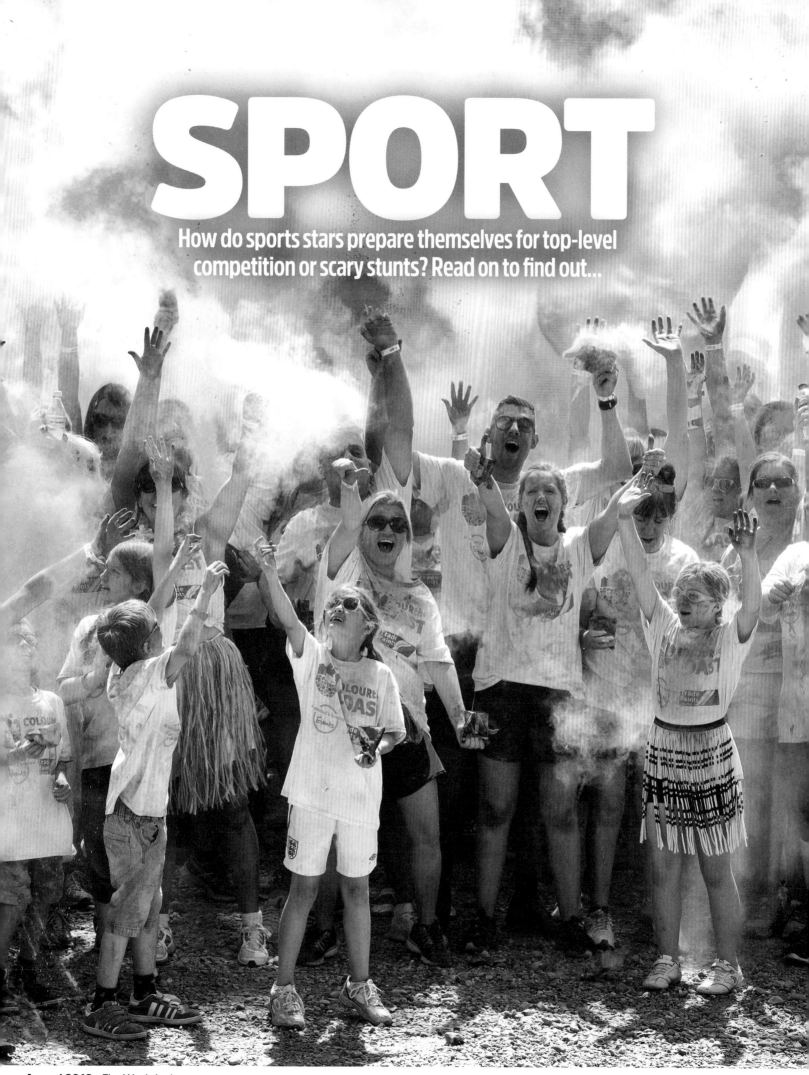

SPORT

How do sports stars prepare themselves for top-level competition or scary stunts? Read on to find out...

The secrets of sport

It requires more than just gruelling training to drive the top sports stars to glory.

What does it take to become one of the top sports stars in the world? If there's one thing Jessica Ennis-Hill, Mo Farah, Bradley Wiggins and Serena Williams have in common, it's almost superhuman reserves of willpower and determination, and of course, hours of training each week. There's more to it than that, however – there's a whole science behind athletic success.

SADDLE SORE
In the Tour de France, roughly 200 cyclists from around the world race more than 2,000 miles in just 23 days.

GREAT GAMES
The Olympic motto is *Citius, Altius, Fortius*, which means faster, higher, stronger.

What is sports science?

The role of sports science is to build an athlete who is strong enough to cope with the demands of top-level training and competition. Sports scientists study everything from what an athlete eats, to how tired they get, to which equipment they use. Thanks to advances in science and technology, the athletes of today are some of the best in history. For example, Jesse Owens won the 1936 Olympic 100-metre sprint in 10.3 seconds. That's pretty fast, but he would have come last in the 2013 World Championship final, which Usain Bolt won in 9.77 seconds. That's partly to do with the different surfaces on which the two athletes ran. What else does it take to be the very best?

TEAMWORK

In some sports, such as tennis and golf, coaches were rare until the 1970s. Today, tennis players such as Andy Murray don't have just one coach but an entire team working for them, including dietitians (experts in diet and nutrition). When it comes to the Olympics, the English Institute of Sport has 250 sports science and medicine staff. It worked with 86% of Team GB's medallists at the 2012 Olympics. The team may include scientists called bio-mechanists who use super-slow-motion cameras to analyse how athletes move, and performance analysts study thousands of hours of film of a player's opponent.

A lot of work goes into every victory.

Coaches help teams.

FOOD

Sports stars have to be careful about what they can and can't eat. Professional cyclists in the Tour de France typically start the race with just 4–5% body fat; an average man has about 18–24%. That's because if two cyclists with equal strength ride up a mountain, the lighter one will have the advantage. However, once the race starts, a cyclist typically gets through 8,000 calories a day. That's the equivalent of about 27 croissants. Cycling teams have their own chef, and eat lots of rice, fish, and white meat.

Cyclists can burn 8,000 calories a day racing.

ng success

Athletes also rely on the latest cutting-edge technology to improve their performance. In the run-up to the 2012 Olympics, the cyclist Sir Chris Hoy wore sensors that delivered data to his trainers about how his body was responding to training. He won two gold medals. In cricket there is now a device that can be attached to the bat so players can track things such as bat speed and angle, which allows them to adjust their technique and improve the way they play.

AND THE REST...

Gymnasts are usually small and light.

HUMBLE BEGINNINGS

The first Fifa World Cup was held in Uruguay in 1930. Only four of the 13 teams taking part came from Europe because it was such a long journey by boat. No British teams entered.

MENTAL PREPARATION

The world's top athletes need to be able to cope with the mental pressure of performing in front of big crowds. That's where psychologists come in. Sports psychologists can help athletes who are anxious, scared of failure or those who might lose their temper during competitions. One of the tools psychologists use is specially designed relaxation techniques.

Experts also believe that, aside from the technology and science, there are other factors, often out of an athlete's control, that determine how successful they are. Evidence suggests that top British athletes are most likely to grow up in medium-sized towns and attend schools in small villages. Body type also plays a part – successful gymnasts and divers are usually small and light. Finally, as more records are broken and the incredible endurance of humans is tested to the limit, some experts think that self-belief is one of the biggest driving forces for athletes – the idea that you can do anything.

Making a splash
Competitors tackle the steeplechase race at the Athletics World Championships in London.

HOT TICKETS
More than 705,000 tickets were sold for London 2017 – more than any World Athletics Championships ever.

Not a day at the beach
Spain's Ana Peleteiro plays with the sand after competing in the triple-jump.

Mo goes for gold
Mo Farah wins the 10,000-metre race on the opening night of the championships.

Best foot forward
Competitors keep their eyes on the prize in the 110-metre hurdles.

Starting blocks
Usain Bolt gets ready to race in the heats of the 100-metre sprint.

BYE-BYE BOLT
Usain Bolt retired after London 2017. In his career he won an amazing eight Olympic golds and 11 World Championship golds.

Sky-high
Brazilian long-jumper Paulo Oliveira takes to the air.

SHOW NO FEAR!

Discover the men and women competing in the most extreme sports in the world.

Wingsuit flying

Wingsuit flying is the sport of gliding through the air like a real-life Batman, wearing what is sometimes called a flying-squirrel suit. The suit's floppy fabric increases the surface area of the pilot's body, allowing it to float and fly. US wingsuit pilot Joe Ridler reached 232.9mph on 23 October 2016, setting the record for the fastest average speed achieved in a wingsuit. A group of 61 wingsuit pilots also took flight together over California, US on 17 October 2015. This is one of the world's most dangerous sports.

Surfing

For centuries, surfing was a part of ancient Polynesian culture, but it took until the 1960s for professional contests to begin. Surfers' skills are tested by their ability to control their surfboard in tough conditions, riding difficult waves and performing manoeuvres. The tube ride is considered the ultimate move; a surfer positions themselves inside a wave as it is breaking over their head. A 23.8-metre wave ridden by Garrett McNamara at Nazaré, Portugal, is recognised as the largest wave ever surfed. Surfing, like all watersports, carries many dangers. Surfers run the risk of collisions, drowning and coming across some dangerous marine life.

Skateboarding

Skateboarding was born in the 1950s, when surfers in California, US, wanted something to do when there weren't any waves. It was originally called "sidewalk surfing". In the 1980s, some of skateboarding's biggest personalities, such as Rodney Mullen and Tony Hawk, hit the scene. Mullen is credited for creating some of the sport's biggest tricks, including the kickflip, where a rider flips their board 360° from the nose to the tail. Skateboarding received the ultimate stamp of approval when it was announced as a sport for the 2020 Olympic Games in Tokyo, Japan.

GNARLY TRICK
Tony Hawk was the first person to land a 900: two-and-a-half mid-air turns on a skateboard.

RED BULL CONTENT POOL

Kitesurfing

Kitesurfing uses the power of the wind through large, parachute-type kites to tow riders across the water on small surfboards. There are many different styles of kiteboarding, including course racing and freestyle. The world record for kitesurfing the longest distance non-stop is held by Francisco Lufinha, who travelled 536 miles from Lisbon in Portugal to the island of Madeira. Nick Jacobsen achieved the highest kite jump in Cape Town, South Africa, reaching 28.6 metres high on 19 February 2017. A course-racing style of kitesurfing was considered by the Olympics authority as a sport to be included in the 2016 Rio games, but it was later cancelled.

DANGER IN THE SKY
In kitesurfing, the word kitemare means an accident or dangerous mishap. Kitemares can be deadly.

BMX racing

WHAT'S IN A NAME?
BMX is the shortened name for bicycle motocross. Motocross involves light motorbikes racing on off-road courses.

With its origins in US dirt-track motor racing, BMX exploded in popularity in the 1980s. The track usually consists of a starting gate for up to eight riders, and a dirt course made of various jumps. BMX racing bikes are simple and strong, with a single gear and usually just a rear brake. It is now an Olympic sport, with Connor Fields of the US and Colombia's Mariana Pajón the current men's and women's champions. London's Olympics in 2012 encouraged more people to take part in the sport in the UK, with new clubs, tracks and competitions springing up all over the country.

Ice climbing

Ice climbing evolved out of rock climbing. Climbers spend hours, or even days, with their faces flat against the side of a glacier or frozen waterfall, using axes and ropes to scale treacherous surfaces. The sport is very dangerous, and avalanches can happen without warning. In 2015, Will Gadd – recognised as one of the world's best ice climbers – became the first person in the world to clamber 47 metres up a partly frozen Niagara Falls, which is on the border between Canada and the US.

A knight in cricket armour

Heather Knight did things the hard way.

Only a select few sports stars each year ever get to lift a world cup trophy as captain. In 2017, Heather Knight joined that elite list when she lifted the Women's Cricket World Cup trophy at Lord's cricket ground in London after beating India in the final. However, Knight, who plays cricket for England, as well as leading Western Storm in the Kia Super League, had to travel a hard road to reach the top.

When she went to play cricket as a child, she was quite often the only girl, and started playing boys cricket for a local club. She remembers bowling out one of the boys in her first game and "him not being very happy about it". She was picked for Devon boys before finally being able to play in girls teams from the age of 13. Although it wasn't a straightforward path, she says she wouldn't have had it any other way. In fact, football had previously been her

favourite sport. She loved watching Arsenal, and played for Plymouth Argyle Ladies, but eventually she decided to give it up. "I'm not the quickest, so cricket took over and I made the right decision," she explains. Another bump in the road came in 2013. "I pretty much ripped my left hamstring off the bone," she remembers. "That meant five months on the sidelines." Instead of feeling sorry for herself, she used this experience to spur her on. "Moments like that make the success more special," she says. "When things go well, you remember those low times because it isn't always that way."

Knight can see the effect her success has had on others. "It's always a nice touch to see lots of girls in the crowd," she says. "You see the look they give you. You can see they look up to you and want to get involved."

 DEDICATED PLAYER
Knight picked Cardiff University over Cambridge University for her science degree because it would allow her to spend more time playing cricket.

Knight (left) plays cricket for England.

TOUGH WEEK
Knight trains five or six days a week and this includes physical and skills work.

Q&A

Heather Knight
The England cricket captain on dealing with nerves and stopping for food.

What does cricket offer young people that other sports don't?
It's the only sport where you stop for a food break. That's something that definitely attracted me as a kid. There's nothing better than being out with your mates playing in the sun. There's always something new to learn.

Who helped you develop as a player?
My parents were instrumental. They encouraged me to keep playing and drove me all around the country. I can't thank them enough.

When have you been most nervous?
I wasn't too bad in the World Cup final; I'm more of a nervous watcher than when I'm in the game. I was most nervous for the first England game I ever played on telly. It was at Adelaide Oval in Australia and I was worried I'd do something stupid.

Did you watch much cricket on TV when you were growing up?
I would watch England Test matches on TV. My favourite player was Marcus Trescothick. I loved watching him

bat. He's from the West Country, where I'm from, and was an opening batsman, which I was growing up.

What's it like playing in the Kia Super League?
There's entertainment at the grounds and it's very colourful. It's great fun for kids. Some of the best players in the world are on those teams.

What would you be doing if you didn't play cricket?
I would've done something quite sciencey, I expect, and been wishing I was playing cricket.

Stories about sport

Get inspired with these tales of sporting fun and glory.

EARLY START
Football star Wayne Rooney wrote a book about his life story when he was just 20 years old.

Books about sports are often inspiring – featuring tales of passion, dedication and overcoming the odds. There are lots of different sports-themed stories out there, so whether you prefer badminton or basketball, cricket or cycling, running or rock-climbing, you can be sure to find something that will appeal to you. Kick off with these five books about young heroes, each of whom have a particular sporting talent and are pursuing their dream. Join them on their journeys of self-discovery as they reach for the stars. You might even be inspired to have a go yourself.

Kick
by Mitch Johnson
(Usborne Books)

Eleven-year-old Budi works in the slums of Indonesia making football boots, but he dreams of one day becoming a football star. Then one unfortunate kick changes everything – and Budi finds himself in danger. The first book from Mitch Johnson, this is a powerful story about hope and inspiration, which will leave you with plenty to think about.

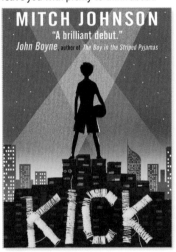

Tall Story
by Candy Gourlay
(Random House Children's Books)

Andi and her half-brother Bernardo love basketball, but while Andi is in the UK, dreaming of playing for the school team, Bernardo is in the Philippines, waiting for the papers he needs to join his family. This is a heartfelt story about how people from different cultures can learn to understand each other.

Flying Fergus
by Sir Chris Hoy and Joanna Nadin. Illustrated by Clare Elsom
(Templar Publishing)

Champion cyclist Sir Chris Hoy has joined forces with author Joanna Nadin and illustrator Clare Elsom to create this fun, cycling-themed adventure series. In the first book, Fergus is disappointed to receive a rusty second-hand bike, but then he discovers that his new bicycle has some rather magical powers...

White Boots
by Noel Streatfeild
(HarperCollins Children's Books)

After an illness, Harriet is advised to take up ice-skating by her doctor. Nervous and unsure at the ice rink, she meets Lalla, a talented and confident young skater. The two girls are soon the best of friends, but before long, Harriet's skating ambitions begin to threaten her friendship with Lalla.

Roller Girl
by Victoria Jamieson
(Puffin Books)

When Astrid discovers roller derby, she falls instantly in love. Soon she's signed up for skate summer camp, but as she struggles with setbacks, friendship dramas and the challenge of staying upright on her skates, will she ever become a real roller girl? This awesome graphic novel will make you want to stand up and cheer for Astrid as she sets out to make her dreams come true.

Wordsearch

 ANSWERS CAN BE FOUND ON PAGES 94–97

Can you find all of these football words and phrases in the grid? Words may be hidden horizontally, vertically or diagonally, and reading either forwards or backwards.

ATTACKER
BICYCLE KICK
CAPTAIN
CLEAN SHEET
CLEARANCE
CLUB
CORNER KICK
CROSSBAR
DEFENDER
DERBY
DRIBBLING
EQUALISER
EXTRA TIME
FINAL WHISTLE
FIRST ELEVEN
FORWARD
FREE KICK
FRIENDLY
FULL-TIME
GOALKEEPER

HAT-TRICK
INJURY TIME
MAN OF THE MATCH
MANAGER
OFFSIDE
OWN GOAL
PASS
PENALTY SHOOTOUT
PITCH
PROMOTION
RED CARD
REFEREE
RELEGATION
SUBSTITUTE
TACKLE
THROW-IN
VOLLEY
WINGER
WORLD CUP
YELLOW CARD

```
J Y W T V U C R O S S B A R L V T W R R
L E Z F W O R L D C U P D A T A C K L E
E P K V S W L R E P E E K L A O G R Y D
R G C B U L C L E A R A N C E R D M L N
M R I T B E G R E B N I W O R H T H D E
A A K R S K P A Y Y O S S R S S A P N F
N P E X T R A T I M E V H N E T O N E E
O Z E T I N J U R Y T I M E T G S E I D
F I R S T E L E V E N O F R E L N N R S
T Z F S U K K L Y H D I I K H T K I F O
H N O I T O M O R P N C J I R T B A W O
E T B X E I F X S A K L L C R B E T S B
M F E B I C Y C L E K I C K L E O P M R
A E Y E L L O W C A R D R I R U W A F R
T U O T O O H S Y T L A N E P A N C O T
C N R E S I L A U Q E G F I D A G U R H
H P U J S A J S Z S T E T A G C O W W L
J E A T T A C K E R R C A E Q W A R A T
F U L L T I M E G S H X R S E R L R R I
R E L E G A T I O N R L E O F F S I D E
```

Sudoku

Place each number from 1–6 exactly once in each row, column and bold-lined 3x2 box. Can you complete the grid and solve the sudoku puzzle?

		2	6		
5	3				
		1	5	3	
	3	5	1		
			3	6	
		6	2		

Code riddles

Each of these words relating to cricket has had each letter replaced by the letter after it in the alphabet (so A becomes B, B becomes C and so on). Can you break the code to find the answers?

CBUTNBO =

TQJOOFS =

JOOJOHT =

Number tower

Place a number in every square to complete the number tower. The value in each square is the sum of the numbers in the two squares directly beneath it.

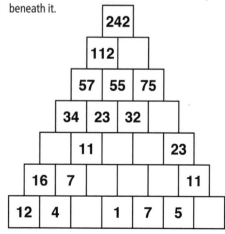

```
            242
          112
        57  55  75
      34  23  32
        11        23
    16  7            11
  12  4      1  7  5
```

Number cross

All the numbers below appear exactly once in the puzzle grid. Can you work out where each one goes? We've placed one number to start you off.

4 numbers
2304
2763
3681
3816
4593
8717

5 numbers
38525
51261
61770
81482

6 numbers
122563
212712
456444
986515

7 numbers
4514155
6975893
8857650
8986543

8 numbers
28483821
42582115
68336446
79784575
80602189
81968343

Grid start: 5 1 2 6 1

Anagrams

Rearrange the scrambled letters to form words relating to tennis.

SNAILBEE
(CLUE: You'll find this at the back of the court)

VEGANDATA
(CLUE: Players want this when the score is deuce)

HERONFAD
(CLUE: A popular style of hitting the ball)

Keyword crossword

Once you have completed the crossword, use the letters in the highlighted boxes to form a word. Write it in the space below the clues.

Across
3. More secure (5)
5. Make something longer by pulling it (7)
6. Extremely precise (5)
8. Opposite of outer (5)
10. Moral (7)
12. A common type of sports shoe (7)
13. Measure of how far down something is (5)
15. Operate a car (5)
16. Feeling (7)
17. Too much of this sweet substance is bad for your teeth (5)

Down
1. Roughly calculated (9)
2. Where you are right now (4)
3. Person who looks after sheep (8)
4. Country whose capital is Paris (6)
7. Mobile ___: communications device (9)
9. Animals that pull Santa's sleigh (8)
11. Kind-hearted (6)
14. Consumes food (4)

Keyword clue: Name of a sport

Spot the difference

Can you find the five differences between these pictures?

HOW TO...
Write a sport report

Here's a fresh way to get in the game.

Do you enjoy watching sports such as athletics, cricket, cycling, football, gymnastics, netball, rugby, swimming, tennis and many others? Why not write a report about an event you have taken part in or seen? *The Week Junior* reveals five top tips to help you create a fun and interesting sport story...

WOW!
The Week Junior covers different sports each week and has even sent readers to write about major events.

Getting started

Write about an event that interests you.

1 For your first attempt at a sport report, write about an event you are interested in and know something about. This will make the writing easier because you will know the basic rules and how the points, scoring system and the winner or winning team is worked out.

2 Keep your writing simple and stick to sentences that will be easy for your reader to understand. The first rule of your report is to tell the reader what the competitor or team you're writing about has won or achieved.

3 Make a note of the key points to include in your story. If you're watching a live event or thinking back to a race or competition in the past, jot down the important things to include. This might be a specific record, a goal or a medal won. Tick off your notes as you include each one in your full report.

4 Sometimes in a report it's good to include something that the winner said about their achievement. This is called a quote. If you've heard or seen a good quote from the people in your story, you can include it if you like.

5 Can you think of a fun headline for your report? This will usually be between four and eight words and should be interesting and make people want to read the story. Have a look at sport reports in *The Week Junior* to give you examples. You can also check out sport websites for more information about events and athletes, which will give you information for your story.

6 If you'd like the chance to get your report published in *The Week Junior*, simply send it to us at *hello@theweekjunior.co.uk*

Over to you

Try writing your first sports report here.

HEADLINE:

RULES OF WRITING
News and sport reports should always include these facts, known as the 5 Ws...
Who is involved?
What happened?
When was the event?
Where did it happen?
Why did it happen?

Sheffield steal victory on the ice

On 9 April, Sheffield Steelers won the Elite Ice Hockey League Playoff final in a dramatic game. They beat Cardiff Devils 6-5 in overtime to win the competition for the fifth time. Cardiff had already won the Elite League and Challenge Cup this year but couldn't win the last, and most important, trophy of the British season.

The Elite League is the highest level of ice hockey in the UK. There are 10 teams that compete, and besides Sheffield Steelers and Cardiff Devils, the other teams are Belfast Giants, Coventry Blaze, Nottingham Panthers, Braehead Clan, Edinburgh Capitals, Dundee Stars, Fife Flyers and Manchester Storm. They play 52 games in total in the league season and Cardiff won 81 points; Belfast were runners-up with 74 points.

The best eight teams then try to win the Playoff trophy. In the semi-finals, Sheffield beat Belfast 2-0 and Cardiff came from two goals down to beat Dundee 4-2. The Playoff final took place at the National Ice Centre in Nottingham. The score was 5-5 at the end of normal time, so the game went to overtime, when the first goal scored won the game. Sheffield's Levi Nelson scored the winner to take the trophy.

How much of this book can you remember?

1 In which country can ancient stepwells be found?

_____

2 What is the name given to the science or art of making maps?

a) Choreography

b) Calligraphy

c) Cartography

a ☐   b ☐   c ☐

3 When did the last train depart from Michigan Central Station?

_____

4 True or false? Ben Fogle says his hardest adventure was rowing across the Atlantic Ocean.

_____

5 In Cornelia Funke's _Dragon Rider_, the Rim of Heaven is located in which mountains?

a) Alps

b) Himalayas

c) Andes

a ☐   b ☐   c ☐

6 What is it called when king penguins shed their feathers?

_____

7 In which year was the first fully synthetic plastic developed?

a) 1807

b) 1907

c) 2007

a ☐   b ☐   c ☐

8 True or false? A ladybird's spots are there to scare predators away.

_____

9 Which type of bird has a horn called a casque?

_____

10 Michael Morpurgo's book _Toto_ is based on which famous magical story?

a) _Harry Potter_

b) _The Chronicles of Narnia_

c) _The Wizard of Oz_

a ☐   b ☐   c ☐

11 True or false? Amy Johnson was the first woman to fly solo from England to Australia.

_____

12 What is the name of Virgin Galactic's spacecraft, which the company hopes will one day carry tourists into space?

_____

13 How high is the surface temperature of KELT-9b, the hottest planet ever found?

a) Less than 2,700°C

b) More than 4,300°C

c) More than 8,200°C

a ☐   b ☐   c ☐

14 Which Irish comedian is also the presenter of the television show, _Robot Wars_?

_____

15 Famous scientist Marie Curie discovered which two elements?

a) Radium and polonium

b) Hydrogen and oxygen

c) Carbon and nitrogen

a ☐   b ☐   c ☐

16 In which year is the next _Guardians of the Galaxy_ film rumoured to be released?

_____

17 True or false? Actors call themselves thespians after king named Thespis who lived in the 6th century BC.

_____

18 Artist Salvador Dalí kept which type of animal as a pet?

a) Anteater

b) Aye-aye

c) Axolotl

a ☐   b ☐   c ☐

19 Julie Tottman was the head animal trainer for which series of famous wizarding films?

_____

20 Paddington Bear comes from which South American country?

a) Chile

b) Peru

c) Argentina

a ☐   b ☐   c ☐

21 True or false? Mario Kart 8 Deluxe came out in 2016.

_____

22 What is it called when computer graphics are overlapped with real-world situations?

a) Fake reality

b) Semi reality

c) Augmented reality

a ☐   b ☐   c ☐

23 In which year was Minecraft released?

_____

24 What is devkit short for?

_____

25 When was the first call made on a mobile phone?

a) 1963

b) 1973

c) 1983

a ☐   b ☐   c ☐

26 What does the Olympic motto _Citius, Altius, Fortius_ mean?

_____

27 True or false? Usain Bolt won eight Olympic gold medals during his career.

_____

28 What was skateboarding originally called?

a) Sidewalk surfing

b) Board surfing

c) Skate surfing

a ☐   b ☐   c ☐

29 Which women's cricket team did England beat to win the 2017 Women's Cricket World Cup trophy?

_____

30 At what age did footballer Wayne Rooney write a book about his life story?

a) 18

b) 19

c) 20

a ☐   b ☐   c ☐

CHECK YOUR ANSWERS
When you've answered all the questions, head to pages 96–97 to find out how many you got right.

WRITE YOUR SCORE HERE

/30

Around the world

Code riddles: California, New York, Florida
Anagrams: Argentina, Ireland, Belgium
Keyword: Germany

2	5	8	1	3	7	6	4	9
6	1	3	2	9	4	8	7	5
4	9	7	6	8	5	2	3	1
3	8	6	4	5	9	1	2	7
1	2	4	8	7	6	5	9	3
9	7	5	3	1	2	4	8	6
5	3	1	9	2	8	7	6	4
7	4	2	5	6	3	9	1	8
8	6	9	7	4	1	3	5	2

Animals and environment

Code riddles: hutch, stable, beehive
Anagrams: chicken, pelican, pigeon
Keyword: recycling

8	2	1	5	3	6	7	9	4
6	7	5	9	2	4	1	8	3
3	9	4	1	7	8	6	2	5
2	5	3	4	9	1	8	6	7
1	6	9	7	8	3	5	4	2
7	4	8	2	6	5	9	3	1
9	3	7	8	1	2	4	5	6
4	1	2	6	5	9	3	7	8
5	8	6	3	4	7	2	1	9

Science and technology

Code riddles: particle, electricity, magnet
Anagrams: ankle, kidneys, stomach
Keyword: chemistry

2	5	1	4	6	3
4	6	3	1	5	2
1	2	4	5	3	6
5	3	6	2	1	4
3	1	2	6	4	5
6	4	5	3	2	1

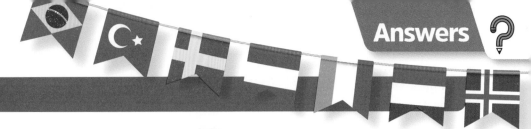

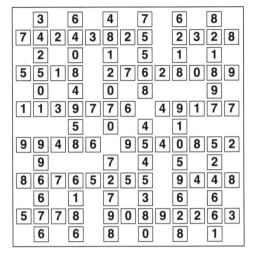

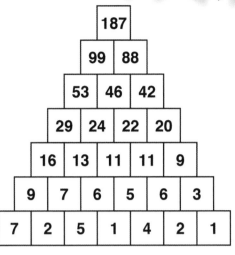

Number pyramid 1:

			187			
		99		88		
	53		46		42	
29		24		22		20
16	13	11	11	9		
9	7	6	5	6	3	
7	2	5	1	4	2	1

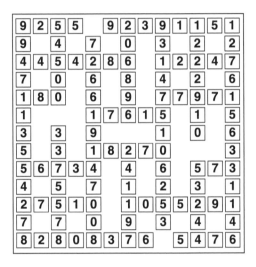

Crossword 2:

Number pyramid 2:

			216			
		101		115		
	46		55		60	
22		24		31		29
13	9	15	16	13		
10	3	6	9	7	6	
8	2	1	5	4	3	3

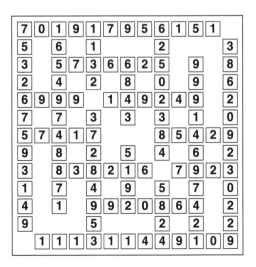

Crossword 3:

Number pyramid 3:

			227			
		97		130		
	47		50		80	
28		19		31		49
19	9	10	21	28		
12	7	2	8	13	15	
6	6	1	1	7	6	9

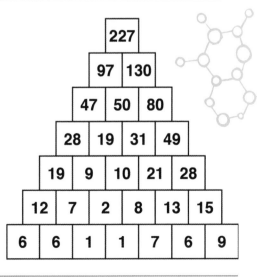

Answers

Arts and entertainment

Code riddles: Roald Dahl, Beatrix Potter, Lewis Carroll
Anagrams: dancer, comedian, impressionist
Keyword: Walliams

6	5	3	1	2	4
2	1	4	6	3	5
3	4	1	2	5	6
5	6	2	3	4	1
4	3	6	5	1	2
1	2	5	4	6	3

On screen

Code riddles: Instagram, Twitter, Facebook
Anagrams: email, password, software
Keyword: gadget

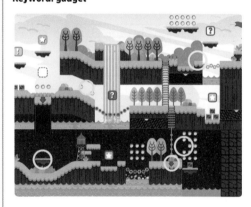

6	2	5	1	3	4
4	3	1	6	2	5
3	5	4	2	1	6
2	1	6	4	5	3
1	4	3	5	6	2
5	6	2	3	4	1

Sport

Code riddles: batsman, spinner, innings
Anagrams: baseline, advantage, forehand
Keyword: athletics

1	4	2	6	5	3
6	5	3	4	1	2
2	6	1	5	3	4
4	3	5	1	2	6
5	2	4	3	6	1
3	1	6	2	4	5

Quiz answers 1 India 2 c) Cartography 3 1988 4 True 5 b) Himalayas 6 Moulting 7 b) 1907 8 True 9 The great hornbill 10 c) *The Wizard of Oz* 11 True 12 Unity 13 b) More than 4,300°C 14 Dara O Briain 15 a) Radium and polonium 16 2020 17 False, Thespis was a poet

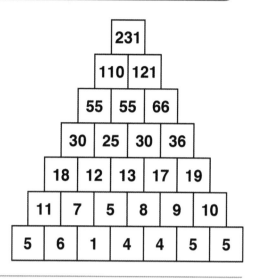

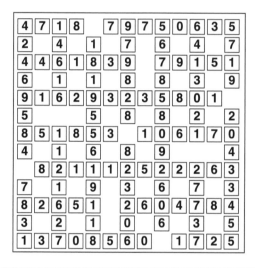
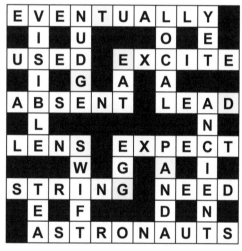

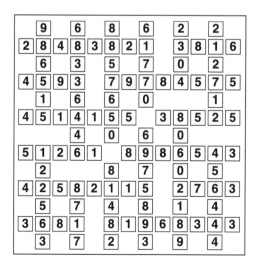

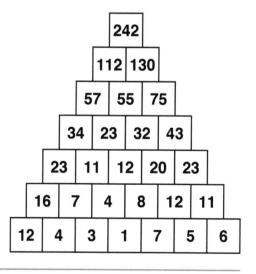

18 a) Anteater **19** *Harry Potter* **20** b) Peru **21** False, it came out in 2017 **22** c) Augmented reality **23** 2009 **24** Development kit
25 b) 1973 **26** Faster, higher, stronger **27** True **28** a) Sidewalk surfing **29** India **30** c) 20